500 ideas for

smallspaces

Kimberley Seldon

easy solutions for living in 1000 square feet or less

Creative Publishing
international

CHANHASSEN, MINNESOTA
www.creativepub.com

Creative Publishing international

Copyright © 2007
Creative Publishing international, Inc.
18705 Lake Drive East
Chanhassen, Minnesota 55317
1-800-328-3895
www.creativepub.com

Printed in China

10 9 8 7 6 5 4 3 2

Library of Congress Cataloging-in-Publication Data

Seldon, Kimberley,
  500 ideas for small spaces : easy solutions for living in 1000 square feet or less / Kimberley Seldon.
      p. cm.
  Summary: "A practical guide featuring 500 real-life remodeling, organizing, and decorating tips for making a small home look and function better"--Provided by publisher.
  ISBN-13: 978-1-58923-301-0 (soft cover)
  ISBN-10: 1-58923-301-8 (soft cover)
  1. Interior decoration. 2. Small rooms--Decoration. 3. Interior decoration. 4. Storage in the home. 5. Small houses. I. Title. II. Title: Five hundred ideas for small spaces.

  NK2117.S59S45 2007
  747'.1--dc22

2007010819

President/CEO: Ken Fund
VP for Sales & Marketing: Peter Ackroyd

Home Improvement Group

Publisher: Bryan Trandem
Managing Editor: Tracy Stanley
Senior Editor: Mark Johanson
Editor: Jennifer Gehlhar

Creative Director: Michele Lanci-Altomare
Senior Design Manager: Brad Springer
Design Managers: Jon Simpson, Mary Rohl

Director of Photography: Tim Himsel
Lead Photographer: Steve Galvin
Photo Coordinators: Julie Caruso, Joanne Wawra
Photo Research: Adrianne Truthe
Shop Manager: Randy Austin

Production Managers: Linda Halls, Laura Hokkanen

Book Designer & Page Layout Artist: Lois Stanfield
Photographer: Joel Schnell
Shop Help: Glenn Austin, John Webb

contents

dream big in small spaces

If you live in a modest-sized home, condo, or apartment, chances are you're keenly aware of the limitations of small-space living. Soaring real estate prices have advanced the proliferation of homes and condos that are smaller and smaller in size, inciting the desire for inventive solutions to cope with space limitations.

Making effective use of space is therefore one of design's most fundamental issues. But don't despair; designers have a stack of tricks for making close quarters appear more spacious and inviting. Dare to dream big, and your rooms can be a triumph of style over size.

—Kimberley Seldon

Ask most teenagers about the function of the living room and you're apt to see a bewildered shrug. Ask them about the duty of a family room on the other hand and watch how quickly confusion turns to confidence. "It's for hanging out and watching TV," they reply. True enough. However, for those who live in small spaces without a dedicated family room, the living room must be used for, er, living.

Whether the occasion is an impromptu movie night, a restful moment with a good book, or a card game with the boys, the living room facilitates lingering and happy gatherings. In other words, it's not just a showplace; it is the true heart of the home.

living rooms

To create comfort in a small living room, choose solid fabrics and use simple patterns for accent pieces. This provides the space with "breathing room," reducing visual chaos. Furniture that does double duty—a sofa that becomes a guest bed, a coffee table that rises to dining height—stretches the living room's functionality.

If budget doesn't allow for a total makeover, is it possible to rearrange, reupholster, or refinish what you already own? Try moving furniture around—a new position frequently brings a new perspective.

By all means, honor family history in this important room by displaying items with personal meaning. Whether it's a child's first watercolor or a selection of seashells collected on vacation, these happy elements invite pleasant reflection and fill your home with joy.

1 In a small living room, where the goal is to create the illusion of more space, paint walls and trim in pale, cool colors such as lavender, cloud blue, or sea green. Cool colors recede from view, making walls feel farther away than they really are.

design tip
Use warm tones such as red and orange to create a space that is intimate, cozy, or dramatic.

2 It's possible to visually erase a room's boundaries—corners, baseboards, and crown moldings—by working with a monochromatic color scheme. Paint the walls and ceiling in an identical shade, and then choose a floor color that's close in value.

3 Paint the ceiling a high-gloss color to add sheen and drama to any room. This works well when the ceiling is in near-perfect condition as high-gloss paint emphasizes imperfections in the drywall.

4 Patterns, which appear on fabrics or wallpaper, take up more visual weight than solid expanses of color. Contemporary rooms usually forgo bold or aggressive patterns in favor of solid-color fabrics on large upholstered pieces. Traditional rooms require a minimum of pattern for authenticity. When pattern is desired, choose subtle color combinations such as those featured in tone-on-tone stripes or damask patterns, and use sparingly.

design tip
If you want to make a small space look cozier, accessorize with bold pattern.

5 Evaluate the scale of furniture before choosing a pattern for upholstery. A dining room chair seat cannot handle a repetitive pattern of large objects. In contrast, a three-seat sofa dotted with a tiny motif is visually overwhelming, and the end result is a dizzy display that detracts from the comfort and beauty of any living room.

6 When creating a floor plan, place the largest pieces of furniture first to signify the premier activity center of the room. Most often the largest piece of furniture faces the room's focal point: a great view, a handsome fireplace, or a television.

design tip
If the living room has a fireplace, it's likely to be the focal point of the room. Emphasize its role by selecting a subtly contrasting color for walls. If the mantle is unattractive and replacing it is not an option, minimize its impact by choosing a wall color that blends with the mantle.

7 Be aware of the room's traffic patterns. When possible, guide pedestrians around (rather than through) conversation areas. Position the main seating area in the room's center to create a traffic perimeter, or place furniture in a tight U-shape in front of the television set.

8 Don't be misled by a room's small scale when it comes to purchasing furniture. A single large piece (or a select few large pieces) actually creates the illusion of spaciousness and provides maximum comfort. In contrast, tiny furniture has the potential to create an unwelcome and uncomfortable appearance.

9 Plan for a primary and secondary activity to take place in the living room, creating a space that supports more than one function. A game center or home office is easily accommodated in a small corner. Or place a rectangular table in a bay window and provide footstools for occasional seating.

design tip

It's preferable to choose an ample two-seat sofa rather than a small three-seat sofa. The slightly smaller sofa allows room for an end table.

10 For maximum comfort, select upholstered sofas and chairs—with narrow arms rather than over-stuffed rolled versions—for main seating. Large arms not only waste available floor space, they also make a room appear "bulky."

design tip
Where space is really tight, choose sofas and chairs without arms.

11 Contemporary settings are ideally suited to the merits of a sectional sofa. This functional, flexible piece of furniture repositions into a variety of permutations with armless versions providing the most flexibility. In addition, the modular units fit effortlessly through narrow doorways and into apartment elevators.

12 Rely on small-scale occasional chairs to provide seating that is used only infrequently. The often small scale of metal garden furniture, for instance, makes it ideal for this purpose. Add comfort to foldup chairs with extra pillows or cushions borrowed from a nearby couch or chair. Perhaps store a few extra throw pillows for the chairs in a nearby chest.

13 In order to visually expand a room's size, designers and architects include "negative" space where possible. Negative space refers to the areas of emptiness that surround an item of furniture, such as the underside of a coffee table. Furniture with legs rather than skirts and chairs with open backs allow light to travel more freely through the space. The end result is a bright, airy setting.

14 Expand the apparent size of a small living room by incorporating reflective surfaces. Wall mirrors are a main consideration; however, don't overlook the current popularity of mirrored furniture such as folding screens, end tables, or coffee tables. Or consider furniture with a high-gloss lacquered finish—another technique for amplifying sheen and light.

design tip

Choose a coffee table with a shelf below the main surface to increase valuable storage and display space.

15 Transparent glass or Lucite furniture is unobtrusive, taking up little visual space within rooms. Choose a clear coffee table to reveal a beautiful carpet beneath or a glass end table to "float" within the space. These see-through options work to produce a feeling of vastness.

16 Nesting tables are the perfect solution for small spaces that are used to host smashing parties! These tables do not take up a lot of space and multiply upon request.

17 Look for furniture that has more than one purpose to increase the functionality of small rooms. A spacious stool or upholstered ottoman becomes a side table with the addition of a sturdy tray or extra seating for those impromptu parties. A drop-leaf table folds up against the wall creating a demilune or semicircular tabletop well suited to display. Pulled away from the wall and opened to full size, the table easily becomes a desk or eating table.

18 If space limitations are really troublesome, try assembling furniture on an angle. This may provide an opportunity to squeeze an extra chair into the seating arrangement.

19 To create a secondary seating group that uses a minimum of space, position a comfortable bench against a free wall. Anchor the seating with an end table and light the area independently with a floor or table lamp. Hang an engaging piece of artwork above and watch guests gravitate to the inviting spot.

design tip

"Value" refers to the lightness or darkness of a color—white has a low value and black has a high value.

20 Determine the ideal location for the television, stereo system, and any other item that requires electricity. Then, if the outlets are not conveniently located, hire an electrician to make the necessary changes. It can be tempting to place these elements where the outlets are located, but this is not always the ideal solution.

21 Custom slipcovers not only increase the life expectancy of upholstered furniture, they also provide flexibility when it comes to style. For example, transform a casual living room into a formal room for sitting with a change of slipcovers. This high-impact transition allows you to customize any space as needed.

design tip
If rerouting outlets is not an option, find discreet tubing at a local home store and place it along a wall to reroute wires while neatly concealing them.

22 Take advantage of space in front of windows to position furniture. A bench or pair of upholstered armchairs coupled with an ottoman creates a cozy spot beside a window for reading. If you have plenty of seating already, place a desk, low bookcase, or other low storage options under a window and still enjoy the natural light and views.

23 Another way to put window space to use is to fasten a ceiling-mounted projection screen above the window, where it can be lowered as needed. Since it's ideal to watch movies in a darkened room, this solution is quite practical for walls with windows.

design tip

If you have a wall with floor-to-ceiling windows, it is fine to put furniture in front of the window, but low furniture—such as a bench—is better as views are not blocked

24 Place a narrow console table behind the sofa if space allows. This serviceable piece of furniture provides an ideal spot for table lamps and collections. In some cases it encourages more intimate conversation groupings, as it requires the sofa to be placed in and away from the wall. Sofa tables are also good transitions between the living room and dining room (or kitchen) when the back of the sofa is turned toward the other room.

25 Locate a round ottoman close to a sofa. Curvy shapes create visual softness and simplify traffic patterns.

26 If privacy is not required, consider leaving windows entirely bare—free from unnecessary layers of fabric.

design tip

Accentuate a great view by choosing draperies in a similar color to walls. This technique provides the least visual disruption and emphasizes the expansiveness of the exterior landscape when viewed beyond the window. In rooms with lots of sunlight, opt for light colors and lightweight fabrics such as sunny sheers or delicate linens.

27 To stretch the perceived size of windows, hang draperies outside the window frame and as high as possible. Again, keep draperies in the same color as walls to emphasize the impact.

design tip
If you prefer a soft, filtered light—like that provided by sheers—consider dual-action blinds/shades—they maintain privacy and shade while the blinds are open, but still provide the horizontal shape to visually widen the room.

28 In a really narrow room, consider shutters or blinds rather than draperies. Their strong horizontal presence visually widens the space. And shutters, unlike draperies, leave floors completely free of obstruction.

29 Humanize the scale of a small living room with high ceilings by painting the ceilings in a slightly darker color than the walls or by applying bead board (wood planks, natural or painted) to the ceiling. Patterns on the ceiling visually lower the ceiling, and when it runs parallel to the room's width it visually widens the space as well.

30 Tall bookshelves, stately armoires, and floor-to-ceiling shelving are just some of the elements that help home-owners utilize vertical space. In lofts or condos—where floor space is often limited to 1,000 square feet or less and air space is often doubled—it's important to take advantage of all available space. Floor-to-ceiling bookcases—as narrow as 12 inches—sufficiently store books, most dishware, and accessories while sacrificing very little floor space.

design tip
Fasten a library ladder to shelves that soar toward the ceiling so you can still access the items with ease.

31 To give bookcases or built-in shelves a greater sense of depth, mirror the backs. Choose display items with care as their form is literally doubled by this technique.

32 Hide storage in plain sight by incorporating trunks, chests, and boxes into rooms with space limitations. Employ a chest or trunk in place of a coffee table, or stack a group of decorative boxes beside the sofa to act as an end table.

design tip

Consider placing flat plastic storage bins beneath a large sofa. These inexpensive organizers are perfect for containing stacks of decorating magazines, CDs, and DVDs.

33 To maximize the visual scale of a room, choose an area carpet that embraces all of the furniture, placing it beneath large pieces such as the sofa and chairs. If you have beautiful wood floors beneath, leave a three- to four-inch perimeter of floor exposed to act as the room's frame so you can still enjoy the wood floor beneath.

34 While most homeowners prefer the expanse of high ceilings, many homes (particularly older homes) leave much to be desired in this category. To distract from a low or awkward ceiling, purchase a lively patterned carpet to provide a stylish distraction underfoot.

design tip
In rooms that are asymmetrical, choose carpeting with a consistent pattern throughout. Avoid carpet with a prominent central medallion because it draws attention to the space irregularities.

35 Increase a room's spacious appearance by forgoing carpets altogether in favor of bare wood, tile, or stone floors. These flooring options are considered cool floors. They tend to be hard, unforgiving, and cold, but they make up for these traits with beauty and sturdiness. They can be visually warmed up depending on the tones chosen.

design tip
If cool floors are not your cup of tea, consider installing wall-to-wall broadloom, which has the added benefit of being extremely comfortable to walk upon.

36 A contrasting color scheme creates drama and excitement. Although this does not enhance the apparent size of the room, it may be desired if the goal is to create a glamorous setting. Furthermore, the contrast brings handsome floors into focus, making them more of a feature. Consider making the contrast between the floor and walls.

37 Consider the merits of a well-placed focal point that extends above eye level, enhancing a sense of "breathing space" within a room. For example, emphasize the height and prominence of a small fireplace with the addition of applied moldings to visually stretch the mantel to the ceiling.

38 Transform an empty stretch of wall into the room's focal point by grouping pictures above a narrow console table. This practice uses very little floor space but provides an arresting focal point in rooms where none exists.

39 Consider displaying only one collection within the living room. For an avid collector this requires a lot of discipline. Keep in mind, the single collection will be most appreciated if this streamlined approach is followed. Reserve other collections for adjacent rooms.

40 Trick the eye into perceiving even small rooms as gallery-like and spacious by framing photographs or paintings with wide mats and large frames. Hang artwork as focal points surrounded by breathing room rather than crowded together.

design tip
Larger mats are often perceived as belonging to more "important" pieces of artwork.

41 An art ledge provides the perfect spot to display a large collection of photography or other artworks all in one concentrated area. This prevents the walls from becoming cluttered with too many pieces. And one shelf means less nails in the walls and less time hanging and leveling each piece.

1. Measure the linear footage of your selected display items.

2. Purchase a shelf that is approximately four inches deep and has a routed groove along the top outside edge (to keep items from slipping off the shelf). Install the shelf along the length of any free wall. Be sure to predrill holes and tap in hollow wall anchors where you cannot hit a stud.

3. Arrange frames on shelf. If the groove is not safely holding the frames in place, add a lip or small rail along the front.

design tip
You'll produce a more disciplined collection by displaying only black-and-white photographs. Consider limiting the theme of photos, too; for example, family members in vacation settings. If you have several collections, rotate photos every six months rather than attempt to display everything at once.

42 A corner fireplace demands a less conventional floor plan. Placing furniture on an angle and filling the room with intense color energizes this small space.

43 Banish room-dulling shadows with a flexible lighting scheme. Rely on a combination of overhead lighting—provided by pot lights and chandeliers—and lower- level lighting from table or floor lamps.

44 A wall-mounted lamp brings reading light to a corner without sacrificing floor space to a side table or standard floor lamp.

45 When selecting lampshades, choose a color that blends with other colors in the room. A pure white lampshade will disrupt a room's visual flow if walls and furnishings are darker in color.

46 Mismatched furniture is instantly unified when treated to a fresh coat of white paint. Because it matches, the room benefits by appearing more spacious. This is an ideal solution to tame and unite flea market or tag sale finds.

design tip
For an authentic vintage feel, paint furniture an aged white such as Ralph Lauren's paint colors Picket Fence (White WW57) or Riviera Terrace (WW50).

47 Link connecting rooms and expand interior views by repeating a signature pattern or color. A dominant pattern may adorn draperies or an occasional chair in the living room and embellish only decorative toss cushions in an adjacent room. Similarly, the same color used on living room walls may be an ideal accent color in adjacent rooms.

48 Many bemoan the lack of adequate storage, but frequently there are leftover spaces that can be summoned to provide additional support.

design tip
Gain extra storage by surrounding an interior door with practical shelving such as columns of bookshelves. Link flanking storage units with a shelf that runs above the doorway to increase storage and create an archway that links to the adjacent room. Such visual connections allow the eye to flow from one room to the next, making the space feel larger.

49 To open up interior views, swap a solid wood door for one with glass panes. French doors are ideally suited to small spaces, where they provide a gracious architectural element often lacking in new homes.

50 Cleverly conceal a television by recessing it within a wall. A large piece of artwork or decorative mirror attached to heavy-duty tracks glides effortlessly over the alcove, hiding the big screen from sight. Or hang a large tapestry from a decorative rod and slide it open to reveal the television. This allows you to transform a formal living room into a casual family room simply by shifting the focus from a fireplace or symmetrically placed sofas, as examples, to the entertainment area.

Case Study

■ In larger homes, the living room is often demoted to infrequent use. Not so with small homes, where every inch of space is utilized. For one young couple, their small living room provided a destination for dinner parties, a cozy room for television watching, and a quiet retreat for reading.

In order to provide for the room's demands, we designed a wall of bookshelves, incorporating the existing fireplace behind a new marble surround. Rather than making the space feel smaller, the feature wall created a sense of depth and gave the room an impressive focus.

Painting the shelves to match the wall color imbued the room with a feeling of spaciousness. A plasma television rests above the new mantel; it is equally situated for casual movie nights and vibrant gatherings.

A sofa extends the full width of the room, capturing maximum seating for the couple's entertaining needs and serving as a comfortable spot that's ideal for napping. Two leather club chairs provide compact seating; nesting tables and a Plexiglas magazine rack are flexible enough to move freely about the room. The camel color story is punctuated with royal blue, seen in pillows and accessories. The midtone color appears fresh and lively in daylight, but deepens to rich caramel by evening, offering two distinct impressions within a single room.

Equal parts social hub and inner sanctum, it's clear today's kitchen has to deliver a lot more than storage space for the fridge. After all, this is where we grab our first cup of coffee, pencil appointments in our calendars, open the mail, and pay the bills. It's where we help the kids with homework. And, whether we like it or not, it's where the party always ends up. Oh—and don't forget about cooking.

kitchens

At one time an efficient kitchen was designed around a work triangle, formed by the location of the refrigerator, sink, and range. Although the distance between major appliances is still a valid consideration, the focus is shifting to work zones—centers for food preparation, baking, eating, office work, and even hobbies. These specialized areas are contributing to a more industrious and per-sonalized kitchen than ever before. Unfortunately, available floor space hasn't always increased to meet these growing demands.

With sensible space planning and creative design choices it's possible to maximize the poten-tial of the kitchen, regardless of its size. The ideas that follow will help you create a personalized kitchen that really sizzles.

51 A single color on walls and cabinetry makes a small kitchen feel substantially larger. If natural light is readily available, choose a warm, pale color as the room's base. Biscuit, stone, blush, and salmon amplify incoming light and maximize the space-expanding effect.

design tip
Monochromatic color schemes—where contrast is minimized—visually enlarge the feel of all rooms, not just the kitchen. This principle works with nearly any color range, from deep khaki to pale pewter.

52 Keep your monochromatic kitchen interesting by introducing pattern, subtle changes in color tones, or texture. For example, select a backsplash that is similar in color to cabinetry and walls, but—to avoid monotony and increase the style impact of plain tiles—choose an interesting pattern, slightly different color tones, or a different texture (such as tile with a glossy surface instead of a matte surface).

53 Continue these space-expanding monochromatic principles by choosing hardware that blends harmoniously with other finishes. Accent crisp white cabinets with soft pewter or brushed nickel. Choose an oil-rubbed bronze or antique gold finish to complete dark wood cabinetry.

54 Forgo traditional hardware altogether in favor of a concealed grip—a hollowed indentation placed at the base of cabinet doors that facilitates opening and closing cupboards. This generates a smooth transition between cabinets. By minimizing visual interruptions, the kitchen appears to be larger.

55 If budget allows, opt for cabinetry that reaches to the ceiling. The highest storage spaces are suitable for infrequently used items such as seasonal tins and baskets.

56 If custom cabinetry is not an option, consider placing large baskets on top of standard cabinets or shelves. This provides extra storage while maintaining an organized appearance.

57 Avoid tripping over recycling boxes by providing storage beneath counters or in nearby closets to accommodate these items.

design tip
Store well-loved and well-worn cookbooks in baskets. Reserve one basket for everything you need to accomplish a fast setup when dining guests pop in unannounced—include the tablecloth or placemats, napkins wrapped around silverware, and centerpiece.

60 Dishwasher and refrigerated drawers as well as panel doors over downsized appliances are clever alternatives to their bulky counterparts, especially if you cook infrequently. It will also free up storage space.

61 Although it's a more expensive option, a refrigerator that is the same depth as cabinetry frees up considerable floor space.

58 To create a streamline kitchen with few visual interruptions, consider hiding large appliances such as the dishwasher and refrigerator behind panels that coordinate with cupboards. If budget restraints make that impossible, paint cabinets a color that blends seamlessly with appliance finishes.

59 Store dinnerware and cutlery near the dishwasher so that it can be emptied quickly and easily.

design tip

If your kitchen feels cramped, it's time to take a good look at your basic cooking needs and then take a look at the appliances that cater to those needs. Standard appliances are often not much more than space eaters in small kitchens. Downsize appliances that sit half empty or that are rarely used.

Case Study

■ I love a challenge. Whether it's a slim budget, an awkward space, or a tight time-line, almost every design project begins with a challenge. In my experience, it's these constraints that often yield the most satisfying results. A recent makeover to the kitchen that serves our busy design firm is a case in point.

Due to its basement location, the old kitchen had low ceilings, awkward window placement, narrow proportions, and badly located ductwork that ran straight through the room's center. In addition, the project had only a modest budget allocated for its completion.

To facilitate occasional catered events I needed to incorporate an island, which severely limited the amount of available floor space. I chose to use premanufactured upper cabinets both above and below the counter, rather than upper cabinets

above the counter and lower cabinets below the counter (the traditional practice). Sound confusing? It's not and it's a good trick to try when space is limited. Standard upper cabinets are only 12 inches deep while their lower counterparts are 24 inches deep. I instantly saved a foot of floor space.

62 To make the most of your cabinet space, store tapered glassware so that every other glass is upside down.

63 Hide small appliances such as coffee grinders, blenders, and food processors inside cabinets to take the strain off limited counter space. Swing-up, glide-out, and pull-down shelves make for easy access and instant use.

64 Enjoy the merits of a small kitchen and forgo space-expanding techniques in favor of choices that emphasize the room's coziness. For instance, to create drama, install high-contrast tiles on the diagonal. Opt for affordable linoleum to provide lots of energy and easy comfort underfoot. Paint cabinets in a deep color such as raspberry, khaki, or chocolate brown for a feeling of comfort. These choices may not make a room feel bigger, but they provide drama and intimacy if that's the goal.

65 Every room, even a small one, requires a focal point. In the kitchen, consider the visual impact of a decorative hood that rises to full ceiling height. There are several techniques to enhance this imposing feature. For painted cabinetry consider an applied molding to adorn its face. Or create a custom look by tiling the decorative hood or facing it in a striking metal exterior such as stainless steel or copper.

66 Free up interior cupboard space and improve the overall aesthetics of the kitchen by creating a still life display. Arrange frequently used bowls, pitchers, and baskets on top of a sideboard or buffet or decorative shelf, and install a plate rail or decorative plate rack under cabinets to stylishly display dishes. This way, they are close at hand when needed.

design tip
To use drawer space most efficiently, arrange frequently used silverware and large cooking utensils in a decorative glass or canister set on the counter.

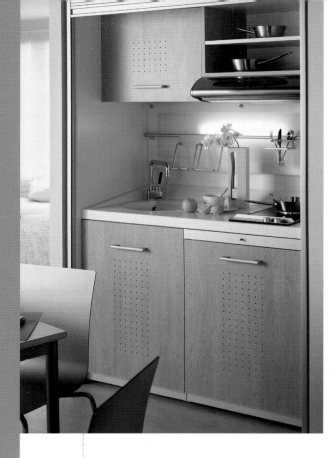

67 Put that wall space behind the sink and stove to use! Consider fastening a single rod along the back wall that accommodates various utensil and towel holders.

68 If you enjoy food shows, consider placing a small television in the kitchen. To avoid added clutter, mount the TV beneath upper cabinets or slide into a side wall that is not used. This also works well for microwaves, electronic can openers, and other appliances.

69 Choose small, portable electronics whenever possible. This includes office items stored in or near the kitchen. To preserve countertop space, for example, choose a laptop rather than a desktop computer. The increased flexibility allows you to move the computer when not in use.

70 For more table space, consider installing a peninsula on a wall within or nearby the kitchen. A peninsula attaches to the wall and extends out for use when lifted and locked into place with hinges. The hinges allow you to fold up the table when not in use.

1. Draw a level line on the wall.

2. Fasten the ledge onto the wall, using wall anchors wherever you cannot hit a stud.

3. Screw hinges onto ledge and flip-up shelf.

71 To stylishly keep track of household paperwork (such as invitations, notices, and children's school notes) place a fabric-covered bulletin board above the desk area. This is a good-looking way to keep the desktop free of clutter.

72 In really tight quarters, create a compact desk area out of a simple wood shelf or ledge. Allow a minimum 18"-deep x 24"-wide wall space to install the cantilevered ledge (no visible support, such as legs). A comfortable stool completes the scene and tucks cleverly beneath the desk when not in use.

design tip

If wall space is available, install shelves above the desktop to hold necessary supplies or, fasten a thin strip of metal to the wall and hang notes on the strip with magnets.

73 Establish a coffee or drink bar in a nearby closet or in a free-standing cabinet set to one end of the kitchen. Supply electrical outlets to accommodate a coffee maker, bean grinder, and kettle. Consider the addition of a minifridge or wine cooler—easily installed beneath a lower cabinet—to keep juice, pop, and water close at hand.

74 With increasing frequency families are choosing to include dining space within the kitchen. Placing the table against a wall keeps the room's center free of clutter.

design tip

Tables with hinged sides that fold down are perfect for increasing your dining table in the event that guests arrive. Such tables are brilliant because they do not require separate storage. For extra seating, consider pulling in benches or chairs from other areas in the house.

75 Where floor space allows, select a round table, as it's less likely to interfere with traffic.

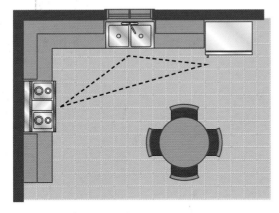

design tip
Look for a round table where leaves are stored beneath the tabletop—thus avoiding the need for additional storage. The addition of leaves in the center of a round table creates an oval table when expanded.

76 Built-ins use the interior spaces in your house that would otherwise not be used while also freeing up your living space. Built-ins increase the depth of the room and allow for more open countertop space.

77 Homeowners may want to consider the merits of a garbage chute, which is relatively easy to build. Allow for an opening of 12" x 12" in the wall to transport waste directly from the kitchen to an outside covered bin. Disguise the chute behind a discreet door that closely matches the wall color and other cabinetry, and install a push latch rather than a knob or pull for opening the door.

78 If a small closet is adjacent to the kitchen, consider converting it to a full-sized pantry. You'll glean extra storage space, possibly a second sink for quick cleanup, and a work space tucked slightly out of the way of visiting company.

79 Get the look of an expensive custom kitchen while expanding available storage capacity with the addition of a freestanding piece of furniture such as an armoire or bookcase. A corner pantry provides plenty of storage without taking up too much floor space.

80 If possible, design the kitchen to include an island that increases available storage space. Even a kitchen trolley (a small free-floating island on wheels) can provide significant storage and countertop space, and it can be moved out of the way when not in use. The second workstation allows two people to comfortably use even a small space. L-shaped kitchens are typically conducive to an island since cabinets are limited to two adjacent walls rather than three.

81 Choose a hard working surface such as granite or a solid surfacing material like Corian or Silestone for countertops.

82 Hang wicker or metal baskets against a wall to capture bills and invitations while saving valuable countertop space.

design tip
Install slim pendant lighting over an island or countertop to provide light where needed without impeding views.

83 If increased workspace is the goal, consider adding or moving a stove, microwave, or sink to the island. Dedicate one side of the island—the side closest to the work zone—to the microwave, and place the sink in the opposite corner. Make sure to include electrical outlets.

84 For compact seating at the island—a favorite spot for children to grab an after school snack—choose bar or counter stools without backs. For comfortable legroom, provide a minimum countertop overhang of 12 inches.

85 Nowhere for Fido to sleep at night? Believe it or not, a small dog bed might be accommodated beneath an island with a minimum 3' x 5' of floor space. Design cabinet doors with open grillwork rather than solid doors, or leave the "doorway" open. Complete the pet palace by placing a comfortable dog bed on the floor and providing toys.

86 Make the most of storage space with lazy Susans or track-mounted bins or glide-out shelves specifically designed for corners. There are even products specifically designed to address difficult storage issues such as those imposed by odd angles, allowing you to make the most of these awkward spaces.

87 Children love to "help" in the kitchen. To keep children preoccupied while you're cooking, consider using bottom drawers for toy storage.

88 Just as the kitchen can be used for nontraditional storage, other spaces are fabulous for bulk kitchen supplies that do not fit neatly (or with easy access) in the kitchen. For example, take advantage of space beneath a staircase for cases of pop, juice, and even cleaning supplies. It's also an ideal spot to hide a large espresso or coffee maker. Place the appliance on a rolling cart for easy access, and put it out of sight when finished.

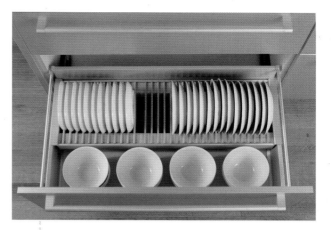

89 It's tempting to buy additional sets of dishes, new utensils, and kitchen appliances as new styles and patterns appear in favorite stores. However, in a small space it's essential to practice discipline. Purchase only one set of quality dishes, for example. Then as space permits, change the look of the main dish set by adding decorative dessert or luncheon plates to the collection.

90 Use a narrow depth (minimum five inches) of wall space to create shelves for spices—the idea is similar to a medicine cabinet. Hide the shelves behind a push latch door, chalkboard, or even a photograph that is hinged to one side of the wall.

design tip
Before buying more stuff for the kitchen, rethink what's required to prepare food and host guests, and then eliminate nonessentials. If the popcorn maker and espresso machine see little action, it may be time to give them to a friend or to charity. And while you're looking through what you do have, examine cookware for flaws and dispose if necessary. This is not only to keep your space limitations in check, but it's also a good safety precaution.

91 Visually enlarge the appearance of the kitchen by replacing solid door panels with glass, perhaps in a sheer color such as pale blue. The only catch: now dishes are on display so a certain amount of discipline is required to keep items looking neat. Yet another option is to use frosted glass. This gives the illusion of sheerness while hiding cabinet contents.

92 To highlight items on display in glass cabinets, consider adding an interior cabinet light. Or flank a window with a pair of glass-front cabinets. Add glass at the sides of the cabinets to allow the sunlight to filter through the interiors and highlight decorative objects.

design tip
If you have a casual country kitchen decorated in French Country, Americana, or Santa Fe style, visually enlarge its appearance by replacing solid door panels with mesh or chicken wire. The open grillwork creates a spacious feel in the kitchen.

design tip

If you do not have a window ledge, consider installing shelves (ideally glass) evenly spaced in front of a sunny window. This technique provides room for potted herbs or an eye-catching collection but it doesn't block incoming light.

93   Although it's not a typical choice for the kitchen, a large mirror amplifies available light and doubles the apparent size of any room. This works best in rooms where natural light is available. Avoid placing a mirror in a dark or dreary corner as it only amplifies its setting.

94   A sunny window ledge can be put to use as display space for a favorite collection or as a gathering spot for potted herbs.

95 Carve out space for a mud-room if there's an exterior entrance into the kitchen. Simple allowances—a change of flooring from hardwood to slate, for instance; a bench with storage; a coat closet or some coat hooks; or a half wall is all that's required to delineate this distinct space.

96 For those who like the kitchen to be off-limits to guests, consider hiding the kitchen completely behind closet doors. That's right! For standard appliances, a minimum width of four and a half feet and a minimum depth of two and a half feet can accommodate a sink, refrigerator, microwave, coffee maker, and shelves. When not in use, shut sliding or louvered doors and your guests won't have a clue what they're missing.

97 A mirrored or highly reflective backsplash casts available light onto countertops and work surfaces, brightening the kitchen considerably. Adding lights under cabinets helps maintain that bright and open feeling even after the sun goes down.

98 Consider hiding extra pots and pans right in the oven. This works especially well for those who cook infrequently.

Key	Part	Dimension
A	(2) Stretcher	¾" × 2½" × 3' poplar
B	(5) Rung	¾" diam. × 18" electrical conduit

99 If you prefer to have pots and pans easily accessible, consider hanging them on a pot rack above an island or open counter space (with a minimum height of 60 inches). Not only does this free up cabinet and counter space, but it also uses valuable—and perhaps otherwise unused—vertical space. Here's how to make your own!

1. After you have drilled one-inch holes in each stretcher, insert J-hooks at each end.

2. Insert the pipe into the compression coupling and tighten the fitting, using a channel-type pliers and adjustable wrench.

3. Finish the rack by plugging the holes in the compression fitting with one-inch chrome-plated furniture caps.

Today's homeowner is embracing the eat-in kitchen with such enthusiasm it's practically triggered a death knell for the dedicated dining room. For some, happy childhood memories revolve around a dining room table: the location of family gatherings and holidays. Indeed, many of our family heirlooms—mother's tea service, grandmother's china—come from the dining room.

The décor of the dining room should blend easily with adjacent rooms, such as the living or family room. It should also reflect your personal

dining rooms

style of entertaining. In many cases, we feel obliged to create very formal dining rooms, even though we entertain on a much more casual scale. Forget everything you think the dining room should be—formal, dark, dramatic, and off-limits—and make it exactly what you want it to be.

Start by assessing your needs. What is the room used for currently? How useful is the dining room when it's not serving its primary purpose? Are there other activities that might take place here? With some thought and planning, you may be able to use the dining room more frequently; increasing the usable square footage of your home or condo.

As our lifestyles becomes more casual, the dining room is perhaps the only bastion of formality; the one room left for occasion. It may be time to reconsider the importance of the dining room in your own family's history—both past and future.

100 As the table is likely to take center stage, consider various options before purchasing. Round tables are cozy and work well in square rooms. They also facilitate the most energetic gatherings, since every person at the table can speak directly to every other person. Keep in mind, an oval table may accommodate only one person at the head of the table during a large dinner party.

101 To eliminate the need for additional storage, choose a table with leaves stored within the table itself. Or purchase a table with hinged sides.

design tip
Allow two feet, six inches of space behind chairs for getting in and out. If possible, allow an ample passageway of about 42 inches for serving access.

102 By its nature a banquette, from the French word for "bench," maximizes floor space, squeezing more seating into tighter proportions. A bay window or unused corner converts easily into coveted dining space with a custom banquette. The absence of chair backs and arms allows the tabletop to rest neatly over available seating. A bench that is 48 inches wide accommodates three diners.

103 If the dining room table also acts as a work surface or game table, choose a square or rectangular shape. This shape is most conducive to other activities.

design tip
Add a three-inch box cushion to the base of a banquet and provide a variety of decorative toss pillows to make this an inviting destination for meal-time and relaxation. Incorporate pullout drawers or a hinged top lid for extra storage.

104 Swap a wood-top table for a glass-top table and enjoy its see-through merits. Anything see-through allows the eye to travel through the space without visual disruptions, making the space feel larger.

105 Traditional dining rooms most often feature rich, dark furniture. Although this is unlikely to make a space feel larger, it doesn't have to close the room in either. The key is to select colors for walls, drapes, and flooring in similar dark tones, thus eliminating contrast and expanding the space visually.

106 Similarly, if dining room furniture is light in color, aim for light flooring and similar tones on walls and draperies. As always, it's contrast that makes a room feel smaller.

107 Extend a sturdy ledge approximately 15 inches deep along the width of the dining room. Use the ledge as needed for a buffet, bookshelf, display, or even an occasional desk.

108 Choose a pedestal table (legs are located in the center) to increase the number of seats that fit around the table. The absence of perimeter legs allows more people to sit comfortably.

design tip
If you have a log home or large wood beams in a small dining room, the logs add a lot of visual weight to the room. To offset that, minimize contrast—going for wall, floor, and furniture in similar value to the beams.

109 Install wood flooring on a diagonal to visually widen a space, or place it vertically along a wall you wish to visually lengthen.

110 Chairs, especially those with high backs, eat up visual and physical space around the dining table. A smart alternative is to provide chairs that tightly mold around the table, thus allowing them to "disappear" when tucked in close to the table.

111 A clever combination of bench and stool seating along the length of a rectangular table allows you to tuck seating beneath the table, freeing up valuable floor space when needed.

design tip
Forgo armchairs in favor of sleek armless chairs and you'll seat more diners.

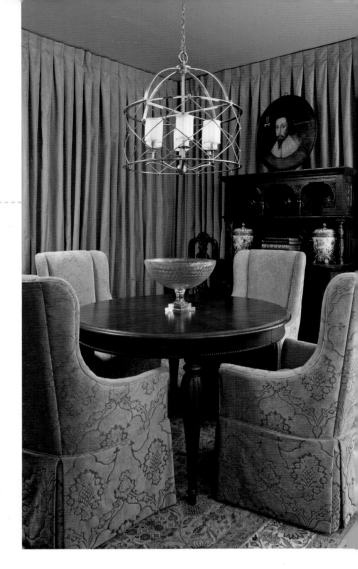

112 Choose dining chairs that transition easily into the living room to provide extra seating when required.

113 Choose reversible dining chair seat cushions. In this way, it's possible to enjoy two distinct looks—one for the dining room and one for the living room, or one for summer and one for winter—without requiring storage for the extra set of cushions.

114 As a general rule, small prints look lost in a big room, and large prints overwhelm a small space. On dining room chairs, aim for a medium-sized pattern that makes a statement but doesn't overwhelm the size of the chair. If a full repeat fits, the pattern will look great.

design tip
If coordinating fabrics seems a difficult task, consider working with a preselected grouping of patterns. Many stores carry such lines, making it simple for the homeowner to mix and match within a controlled grouping.

115 While dark upholstery grants importance to seating, it may make a room feel smaller—just like dark furniture (as described earlier). To diminish this effect, paint walls in a similar color to the upholstery, eliminating contrast and enhancing the room's perceived size.

116 It's a natural choice to incorporate carpet or an area rug under the dining table, as it improves sound absorption. To add an area rug to your dining room, choose the largest size possible. Not only does the room appear larger, it's also easier to slide chairs in and out from beneath the table without getting caught on the edges of the rug.

design tip
Patterned carpets are highly practical, hiding a multitude of imperfections from wear and tear, foot traffic, and, well, the inevitable food and drink slips and spills.

117 The right flooring choice accentuates a room's size, making it appear larger. Opt for flooring in a single color, avoiding pattern. If tile is used, select a grout color that blends seamlessly. Avoid the creation of a textile border, which emphasizes a room's boundaries.

118 If solid doors are blocking views between the dining room and living room, remove them or replace with French doors. Both options create more spacious views.

119 Replace a solid door with a pocket (above) or sliding door (below) to free up available floor space.

design tip
French doors are an inviting way to join two rooms. They generate a strong, open feeling so they should be used carefully. Traditionally they tie together two public spaces.

120 Use sliding doors or simple room partitions made of translucent material, like frosted or beveled glass. The translucent glass allows rooms to share light while maintaining a sense of boundaries that help define rooms.

121 Create a pass-through between the dining room and kitchen to open up interior vistas. Add a stone ledge and it can double as a serving counter .

122 Traditionally more dramatic than other spaces in the home, the dining room is often called upon for evening entertainment. For this reason, it may be warranted to choose textiles with bold patterns and combine them more liberally than in other rooms.

123 Red is definitely not a space-expanding color, but it is ideal for drama. To give a small space big personality, abandon yourself to rich, deep color and celebrate the intimacy and drama of the room.

design tip

Reds to dazzle: Farrow & Ball's Eating Room Red is a deep, rich raspberry; Benjamin Moore's Georgian Red is a traditional brick red ideal for dining rooms and front doors; Sherwin-Williams's Gypsy Red is true red with real impact; Ralph Lauren's Balmoral Red is a decadent dark plum color.

124 Whenever possible, choose midtone wall colors for rooms with dual functions. In this way a room takes on two distinct looks—in daytime the color appears softer, but by evening it deepens to a duskier shade.

design tip

A few favorite midtone colors are ICI's Misty Evening #30BG 64/036, a sultry gray blue; Farrow & Ball's Archive No. 227, the perfect stone; and Benjamin Moore's CC-120, a rich camel color.

125 Elaborate draperies are frequently part of the dining room décor. To emphasize draperies as the focal point, make them bold. This also helps to distract from imperfect views out the window. If hung at the far end of a room, draperies visually expand the dining room area. A long rectangular table perpendicular to the window helps draw the eye toward the window, thus enhancing the perceived space even more.

126 When a great view is present, select drapery fabrics to match wall color. This technique pulls the view into focus, making it part of the room, and as a result the room appears larger.

127 To create two distinct seasonal looks in the dining room—one for summer and one for winter, for example—consider making draperies with a different fabric on each side. Flip the drapes as the seasons dictate.

128 For draperies, select a grommet heading (where the pole threads through a permanent opening at the top) or "hidden" heading (where the hooks attach from the top of the drapes onto a hospital track on the ceiling).

129 For dining rooms that lack windows, consider adding paneled mirrors to replicate the space-expanding and bright feel of windows.

130 Striped wallpaper is effective at stretching the perceived height or width of a room. Choose an elegant pattern for the dining room and run the stripes vertically (to expand height) or horizontally (to expand width). The same effect is possible with decorative paint techniques.

design tip
Choose a stripe that's no less than one and a half inches wide and no more than three inches wide.

131 Mirror the length of a wall in the dining room and double the perceived depth of the room. If the mirrored wall is adjacent to a window, it will amplify sunlight during the day as well.

132 Add visual depth to the dining room by papering walls in textured pattern. If the goal is to create the appearance of a large room, avoid sharp contrast.

133 Take advantage of a recess or large pantry closet for a dining area.

design tip

When designing a room with dark wall color, it's best to avoid painting trim and moldings in pure white. Pure white is glaring and harsh, and the high contrast emphasizes the confines of the room; this in turn draws attention to space limitations.

134 Purchase a bar cart on wheels to serve the dining room and adjacent living room and kitchen. A cart with shelving below also serves as storage. Some versions have a built-in stemware rack for storing wine glasses.

135 Many dining rooms have a buffet to provide storage and facilitate serving. If the buffet is short, consider placing open shelves above to hold additional dishware, glassware, or display items.

136 Place a table, approximately 11 inches deep, against the longest wall. Create a tailored skirt to effectively hide everything beneath the surface. Fasten with Velcro for easy access.

2. Place self-adhesive Velcro on the backside of a purchased table skirt. Reinforce with a simple stitch.

1. Measure the height and width of the area you want to cover.

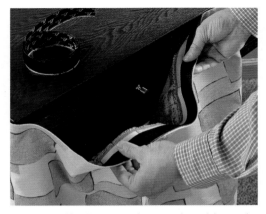

3. Place self-adhesive Velcro on the table, and then simply press the skirt onto the Velcro.

137 If the dining area features a storage closet, replace its solid door with a glass-front door. Add lighting and you'll create a dynamic display area for dishes and glassware.

138 Consider cove lighting, uplights, rope lights, and bookshelf lights to bring drama to furnishings. These light sources enhance the mood of an intimate and dramatic dining space.

139 A central light fixture is frequently seen as the focal point of the dining room. An extravagant crystal chandelier takes up relatively little visual space as it throws light and provides some transparency. In contrast, an opaque barrel shade, popular in many contemporary interiors, disrupts visual flow.

140 Narrow pendants bring light where it's needed without blocking views.

141 Include decorative table lamps on a buffet if room allows. To free up buffet space, install sconces on the wall.

142 Embrace artwork in the dining room, where lingering guests will enjoy its impact. Make sure to light important pieces.

143 While a ceiling-mounted puck light shines directly onto top shelves, its effectiveness diminishes with lower shelves. Install a library light or sconce, which sits outside of the niche, to light the front of all shelves. The added light removes shadows, and this enhances the size of perceived space.

144 Enjoy music throughout your home or condo without purchasing large systems for every room. Many music systems can be routed to infiltrate every room in the house through a centralized entertainment system.

145 Maintain "breathing room" in small spaces by keeping clutter to a minimum. However, you needn't sacrifice impact. Stay away from dotting the room with multiple small objects and aim for a few big impact display items.

design tip
If you're really disciplined, choose one high-impact piece in the dining room to serve as a focal point. This ultimately distracts the eye from the tight quarters.

146 When it's desirable to display a variety of collectibles, unify the exhibit with a single color or color family. For example, a collection of pale blue decorative objects combines to create a single large visual impact.

design tip
Unifying color allows the eye to focus on interesting shapes of various objects, giving them more visual importance.

147 Line the interior of bookshelves with wallpaper. A marbled finish or medium-sized motif creates a handsome and striking backdrop to favorite books and collections. The added layer emphasizes the importance of these objects.

148 When budget allows, wall-to-wall built-ins are ideal for storage.

design tip
Provide a stone shelf at table height within a built-in and it can be used as a serving counter.

149 Purchase quality cookware, tableware, and linens. Accessories go a long way—and a beautiful presentation distracts from the tight size of a room.

150 Dedicated tabletop displays (dining table centerpieces, for example) are ultimately storage stealers, because they have to be stored somewhere when not in use. Instead, use items you already own in imaginative ways. For example, pull some candles from a nearby mantel or fruit baskets from the kitchen to double as displays.

151 Remove clocks and calendars from the dining room to create a calm and timeless dining experience. It also saves space!

Case Study

dining in the library

■ In my opinion, two of the finest things life has to offer are great literature and sharing a gourmet meal (preferably one I didn't have to cook) with good friends. This gracious dining room manages to accommodate both with singular success.

One of the keys to comingling success lies in providing adequate and efficient storage. In this setting, the built-in bookshelves are raised to full ceiling height, taking advantage of every bit of available storage space. Closed storage hides necessities such as dishes and serving platters or, when the space is shared, the detritus of office work. The open storage provides endless opportunity for styling and display. A collection of books is interspersed with porcelain and other collectibles.

Paintings hang at the face of the bookshelves to create a sense of depth and movement and to free up shelf space. The travertine counter in the center acts as a buffet and serving counter, and keeps glass jars filled with flatware close at hand. The mirrored back reflects light, allowing glassware to sparkle.

Painted in a deep brown, the bookshelves are a dramatic backdrop to the formal English dining table. A Beacon Hill damask featuring swirls of chocolate and gold resides on Regency chairs. Upholstered seating provides a comfortable incentive for guests to linger over dinner conversations. It also accommodates quiet study sessions or an afternoon of work.

It used to be that extraordinary design features were reserved for living and dining rooms presumably because this is where they could be admired. In contrast, today's homeowner craves private rooms that pamper, with the bathroom receiving its fair share of upgrades. In fact, you'd hardly recognize this sparkling, modern room from its formerly pragmatic self—even from 20 years ago. State-of-the-art amenities such as rain showers, whirlpools, steam showers, and televisions are making their way into the smallest bathrooms, proving that luxury is attainable at every size. And, thanks to savvy retailers, these upgrades are available in nearly every price point as well.

bathrooms

Let's say you've finally decided to bring a fresh, contemporary feel to your bathroom. That's great, but where to start? A bathroom makeover can be as simple as adding a fresh coat of paint, installing new lighting fixtures, and purchasing new towels, or as detailed as a renovation rescue.

One good place to start the renovating process is to consider what works and what doesn't work in your current situation. It's surprising how many times people renovate and then recreate the same old problems. In general, provide ample storage, make comfort a top priority, and incorporate flexible lighting.

Finally, bring in the accessories! Add scented candles, fragrant soaps, and fresh flowers. Thick and luxurious bath towels are a must.

152 By working with a monochromatic color scheme—variations of one family of hues—it's possible to create an illusion of vastness, even in a small bath. To keep the look current, incorporate judicious hits of color: a selection of pale blue towels or a collection of shell pink toiletries, for instance.

153 Although a majority of homeowners prefer the serenity of an all-white bath and certainly admire its space-enhancing influence, many find pure white too harsh for comfort. By combining warm whites—from eggshell to ecru to cream—it's possible to stave off coolness in favor of luxurious warmth.

154 If you do opt for the space-enhancing effects of an all-white bath, consider anchoring the room with a dark, dramatic floor.

155 Even a tiny bathroom deserves to dazzle. Paint walls in a pearl or semigloss finish, or consider using tiles with a metallic sheen and watch them come to life.

156 A wall of delicate mosaic tiles makes a feature of a striking vanity or gorgeous faucets. Choose a color palette that is slightly lighter or darker than the walls to emphasize this feature without disrupting visual flow.

157 To enlarge perceived space, avoid high contrast grout around tiles. Instead, choose a grout color that most closely matches the color of the tiles.

158 It's perfectly fine to make decorating choices that enhance the apparent size of a room, but this will rarely be the only focus, particularly in a bathroom where matters of function and comfort take priority. For your bathroom, consider flattering color combinations such as taupe and pink, or salmon and tan for their ability to enhance many skin tones. As always, minimal contrast makes a space feel larger.

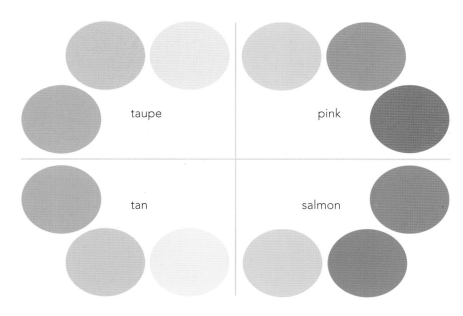

taupe

pink

tan

salmon

159 If your current bathroom has dark cabinets, it's likely they are making the room feel smaller. Give existing cabinets a fresh look with some elbow grease and paint. Of course, with any painting project it's essential to remove the finish from cabinets before priming and painting.

1. Unfasten the hinge screws and remove the cabinet doors from the frames. Place the cabinet doors on a bench and completely remove the hinges.

2. Set the doors on a table and sand them with an orbital sander and 150-grit sandpaper. Wipe away the sanding dust with a tack cloth. Give the doors a coat of primer.

3. Using a trim brush, paint the inside of each door. Paint the center panel first, then the rails, and finally the stiles. When the paint has dried, paint the other side of each door. Paint the door fronts using a tapered sash brush.

160 Although shutters are a streamline choice and well suited to small spaces, a bathroom frequently benefits from the warmth and acoustic buffering textiles provide.

161 Tailored Roman blinds or relaxed blinds also soften a bathroom's hard edges. Choose fabrics to coordinate closely with wall color, allowing visual flow to remain undisturbed.

162 The most interesting window treatments are created using architectural salvage. Mount a stained glass window in front of an existing window to fill the room with color. Or install a section of wrought iron gate in front of the window. This solution provides a modest amount of privacy without being heavy and cluttering the room visually.

163 To provide the greatest feeling of spaciousness in a small bathroom avoid "dotting" the room with color. Shower curtains, if allowed to dominate, are frequently the biggest offenders. Choose a shower curtain that is slightly darker or lighter than the wall color. For really tiny bathrooms, consider an opaque or clear curtain. Gain interest with a decorative detail such as a tassel.

164 If your small bathroom doesn't have a window, you know all too well how stuffy it can feel. Consider adding a mural, such as a landscape scene that allows the eye to view into the distance. Another option would be to paint a trompe l'oeil (fool the eye), an extremely realistic mural, of a window and a scene out the window.

design tip
Ready-made shower curtains often ride too high above the floor. To remedy, add a six inch to nine inch hem to the bottom of the shower curtain.

165 To establish a single focal point in the bathroom, consider adding a gorgeous backsplash or an ornate mirror.

166 A pedestal sink frees up floor space and allows the eye to travel through a room unimpeded.

167 Be consistent in terms of style and finish when selecting hardware. Choose brass or oil-rubbed bronze in traditional settings. Chrome or brushed nickel is effective for contemporary rooms. Mixing and matching only draws attention to the shifts, disrupting continuity and visual flow.

design tip

Be frank with retail suppliers and discuss the small square footage requirements. It may be possible to purchase ends of lines or samples at a reduced rate.

168 A lack of space needn't impede your beauty routine. Architectural salvage may provide a compact solution. A sculptural bracket formerly used on the exterior of a building is an ideal ledge to hold makeup, brushes, and a mirror. Slide a narrow bench beneath to provide seating without compromising available floor space.

169 Use corner spaces for storage. Consider adding hinges to one side of drawers to allow them to swing toward the center of the room for easy access.

170 To save on floor space, install a slim 18-inches-deep vanity instead of the standard 24-inch depth.

171 A small bathroom has a distinct advantage when it comes to incorporating extravagant materials. After all, even expensive options are affordable in small quantities. Hand-painted wallpaper, stone countertops, hardwood floors, and Italian glass tile may all be within reach.

174 Awkward and cumbersome overhead beams are part and parcel for older homes. For visual clarity, hide the beams behind an attractive arch. No one will suspect what lies beneath the architectural feature.

172 Many of today's home-owners are opting for privacy between the toilet and the rest of the bathroom. When space is limited, it isn't always possible o dedicate an independent room to the toilet. However, privacy can be achieved by placing a wall or sheet of tempered the rest of the room. Choose frosted glass to enhance the seclusion.

173 Capturing space beneath a sloping ceiling is always a challenge. It's sometimes possible to tuck a sink or shower beneath the eaves. Make sure to measure the height allowance and provide a minimum clearance of six feet (provided you are not taller).

175 Occasionally a bathroom is so cramped even a standard door swing sacrifices too much floor space. In that case, consider replacing the standard door with a pocket door, which tucks discreetly out of sight. Contact a building professional to discuss the project.

176 Another option is to replace the standard door with two doors (or a single bifold door), effectively cutting the intrusion in half.

177 Most often used commercially, a wall-hung toilet frees up floor space and contributes to a feeling of spaciousness.

178 A recent trend to incorporate furniture into the bathroom means it's finally becoming a room in its own right. An armoire can take the place of a more traditional linen cupboard, while providing a small bathroom with an interesting focal point.

179 Traditional baths favor a piece of antique furniture such as a bergère. Place a Louis XVI gilded chair beside the tub to hold towels, or use a marble-topped gueridon table to display fine toiletries.

180 For the bathroom, consider the merits of woven cane seating or even a metal chair. The semisolid surface is an excellent choice for small spaces, and it won't impede views from a great floor.

design tip
A decorative tray corrals a selection of bath essentials such as oil, soap, and lotion.

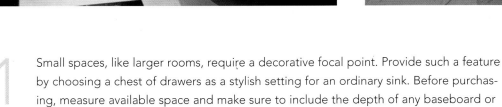

181

Small spaces, like larger rooms, require a decorative focal point. Provide such a feature by choosing a chest of drawers as a stylish setting for an ordinary sink. Before purchasing, measure available space and make sure to include the depth of any baseboard or chair rail. In some cases, it's possible to decrease the depth of a piece of furniture by removing its backside—including the legs—and installing the unit directly against the wall.

design tip

If the vanity is wedged between two walls, it's possible to save money by sourcing a piece of furniture that is damaged. While the front surface must be pristine, the sides and back remain out of sight. In some cases even the top is replaced with a piece of stone. On occasion, store owners keep a small inventory of damaged or sale items that are ideal candidates for this purpose.

182 Tuck a footstool beneath an open vanity to provide compact seating in tight quarters.

design tip
Young moms know the bathroom may be the only refuge in the house. If space permits, a comfortable chair, ottoman, and reading lamp create an ideal location for "checking out," if only for a brief time.

183 If your bathroom is too small for a traditional chair, pull in a comfortable bench or ottoman for extra seating. This also serves as a perfect perch for towels and toiletries. Use terry cloth as a serviceable slipcover and you never have to worry about getting lotion on it.

184 If the vanity is seven feet long or longer, consider building tall storage units on either side of the sink, taking advantage of vertical storage space. Keep the storage towers to a 10 inch depth to avoid a claustrophobic feeling.

185 If a renovation allows for a sunken bathtub, this feature enhances a feeling of spaciousness, freeing the room from clutter at eye level.

186 The front of a radiator cover is an ideal spot to place the towel bar. Hanging towels are warmed by the heat, and the previously unused space is put to service. For a more formal look, consider providing the radiator cover with a marble top.

design tip
To gain extra storage, consider extending the cover around a radiator from wall-to-wall. The storage space behind can be accessed with cabinet doors, and the top is now a functional shelf.

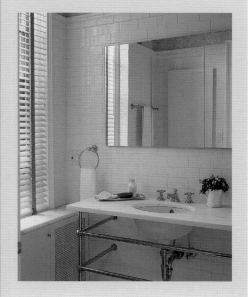

187 Take advantage of space behind the door to hold towels, robes, a full-length mirror, or even a narrow shelf.

188 Rather than place the shower door handle in the standard vertical position, consider positioning it horizontally. In this way, you'll create an extra towel bar right where it's required.

189 Mount or lean a ladder on the wall to supply storage for towels and robes, alleviating strain on drawers.

190 Utilize the exposed side of any cabinetry for a towel bar.

191   Dormer windows often create space that is difficult to utilize. In the bathroom, use the space for a series of built-in drawers to provide the much needed storage small spaces frequently lack.

192   To free up space at counter level, install a narrow shelf 12 inches above the counter. Any shelf will do. Glass shelves maintain a sense of openness. To make the shelf more of a focal point, consider a handsome marble such as gray and white Bianca Carrerra and install a beautiful backsplash on the wall between the countertop and shelf. Use the ledge to display a series of candles or perfume bottles.

193 Create a tower of storage with an open shelf étagère—it is ideal for holding rolled up towels, baskets, and attractive bottles or display items. Consider the merits of a pair of étagère or shelving units flanking the vanity. The forced symmetry adds a note of elegance to the room, creating a sense of order.

194 Minimize visual clutter by keeping toiletries out of sight. Traditional storage is found inside vanities or built-in cabinets. However, a narrow storage unit or cabinet can also be placed over the toilet or wherever available wall space allows.

195 The addition of dividers makes even small storage drawers more efficient. Organize nail polish, jewelry, hair clips, and makeup to speed up morning routines.

196 To streamline dressing, consider placing lingerie drawers in the bathroom itself. Undergarments, socks, and pajamas are excellent candidates to store here. For couples, this is particularly wise when one person wakes much earlier than the other.

197 Extend the depth of a windowsill and create a ledge that's ideal for displaying bath products or decorative bottles.

198 When additional space is available at the foot of the bathtub, harness its storage capabilities with built-in storage from tub surface to ceiling. Store toiletries, towels, or beauty supplies close at hand.

199 If the bathtub sits unused all year long and you have a separate shower area, consider converting it into valuable storage. Install a sturdy rod to hang clothing or build shelves against the longest wall. Hide its contents with floor-to-ceiling draperies.

201 Don't allow cramped quarters to dampen your enthusiasm for creating a space that's uniquely yours. Some homeowners are opting for a mini-refrigerator in the en suite, keeping that bottle of sparkling water close at hand. This is also an excellent idea for storing some medications, lotions, and tonics. The top of the minifridge adds extra countertop space for storage as well.

202 As a general rule, the larger the size of the mirror, the larger the room looks. Opt for a wall-to-wall mirror to expand the appearance of even the tiniest bathroom.

200 A modest-sized television placed discreetly in the bathroom may help you keep up to speed on your favorite television show. If you love a long soak in the tub, consider placing the television within a cabinet at the foot of the bathtub—an indulgent location for TV viewing.

design tip
Make sure to consult a qualified electrician to ensure proper safety measures are followed when installing electronics in the bathroom.

203 When renovating, look for storage opportunities that can be found between wall joists. These "open" areas may be easily converted into hidden niches, ideal for hiding valuables such as jewelry.

design tip
When decorating the bathroom, choose your most uniquely designed products to feature. Many stylish bottles make for perfect display items—not only is it interesting art, but it serves a practical purpose in your day-to-day life. The idea is to feature items you know you'll use instead of stagnant items that will collect dust and steal storage or display space.

204 A good lighting plan is essential, particularly in the bathroom where beauty routines require clear vision. Begin by eliminating shadows with warm incandescent lighting in the form of ceiling fixtures or pot lights. Remember that dark shadows make any room feel smaller and oppressive.

205 To provide the most flattering light for applying makeup or trimming facial hair, you'll want to place light near the face. A pair of sconces flanking a makeup mirror is ideal.

206 Another way to bring light near the face is to set a lamp on the vanity surface.

design tip
To conceal a table lamp cord, drill a small hole through the countertop and allow access to an electrical outlet inside the vanity.

Case Study

■ Although every bathroom in a home is important, the en suite functions as a private retreat, allowing homeowners to luxuriate in the personal pleasures of pampering and relaxing. During a bedroom renovation, my client bemoaned her lack of just such a space. With only one bathroom serving the couple and their three children, she felt she had no privacy.

The bedroom itself was small and provided no obvious solution. However, by confiscating an adjacent closet in her daughter's bedroom, we were able to create a small but luxurious en suite. The improved footprint accommodates two sinks, a modest-sized shower, and a toilet beside a half wall (the half wall adds privacy). But more importantly, it provides a little solitude in an otherwise busy household.

Powder rooms

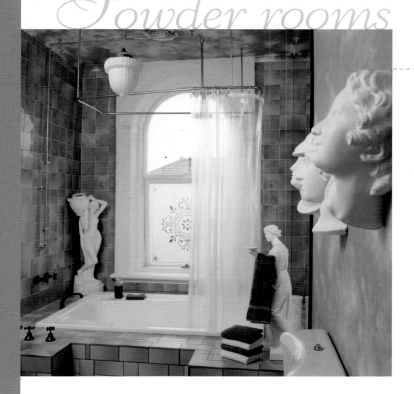

207 Occasionally designers will break all the rules and go for large-scale drama within a small room. The powder room, as it's used for short periods of time, is an ideal location to try such an approach. A bold wallpaper or dramatic paint treatment sets a lively backdrop.

design tip

Take the bold color onto the ceiling as well. The resulting drama creates a welcome distraction from the confines of a tiny space.

208 Although a small powder room can enjoy high-impact pattern, it's best to avoid small allover patterns because they quickly feel monotonous. Good choices include scenic patterns, geometric designs, and classic florals.

209 Lay a tile or wood floor on the diagonal. This pattern helps to stretch perceived space.

210 If flooring is uninteresting or tired looking, choose an area carpet that covers nearly all of the available floor space. As always, minimize contrast in the room by choosing a rug that blends with its surroundings and the space will feel larger.

211 The smallest powder rooms may benefit from a space-saving resource of a corner lavatory and/or corner sink.

212 Paint baseboards and crown moldings in the same color as the walls if the goal is to visually broaden the room.

213 To visually enlarge an ultra-small space, opt for a single color from floor to ceiling.

design tip
To designers, "bold" means daring and exciting—it is a term associated with deep and rich or bright colors. "Dramatic" describes a room that is dark and sultry, perhaps painted in a dark shade such as red or chocolate brown.

Large or small, the bedroom has become a multi-functional space, used for much more than just sleeping. A well-designed bedroom is a place for stillness; it is a sanctuary for resting and dreaming, comfort and escape. Surrounded by gentle lighting and soft, luxurious furnishings, the ideal bedroom revives body and soul.

While many people tend to focus on making small spaces feel larger, the bedroom is the perfect room to aim for intimacy and comfort—feelings that are actually enhanced by a smaller footprint.

bedrooms

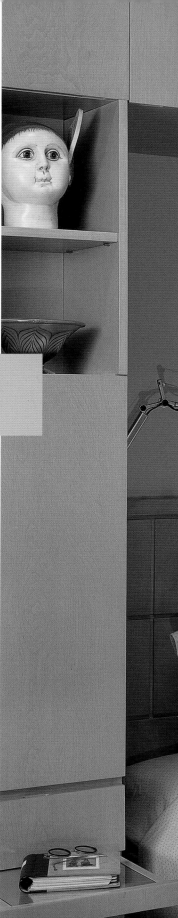

Regardless of space limitations, the bed is the room's focal point. A solid four-poster bed is a handsome and romantic choice while a low bed with little ornament is ideal for a modern or Zen interior. Of course, the most beautiful bed in the world is only as comfortable as its essential components: the mattress and bedding.

In small bedrooms, it's almost always advisable to embrace the confines of space and create an intimate, cozy environment. Explore rich color combinations such as chocolate and blue or charcoal and green. Wrap walls in warm, midtone neutrals and accent the bed with richly textured pattern. Toss a luxurious throw at the foot of the bed and surround yourself with artworks and photos of personal meaning. One word of caution: get it right and you may be tempted to phone in sick Monday morning!

214 Small bedrooms appear larger when the head of the bed is positioned against the longest wall, preferably away from the door.

215 Forgo the footboard to save floor space.

216 Upholstered headboards take up very little space and are comfortable for those who love to read in bed. Choose a fabric color that blends with the wall color to create a feeling of spaciousness.

217 For long, narrow bedrooms, place the bed in the corner of the room. The length of the bed rests against the longest wall, facing into the room's center (not on an angle). This layout accommodates a nightstand at one side of the bed, rather than both.

218 It may be necessary to partially block windows in rooms that are really pressed for space. If so, a bed can exist in front of a window, as can a chest of drawers. At night, closed drapes provide a lovely backdrop.

219 Even small spaces demand comfort. In a tiny bedroom, choose a generous size bed to ensure a good night's sleep.

220 Consider a Murphy bed, which disappears fully into the wall, for really small bedrooms. Out of the way, the Murphy bed frees up floor space and allows the room to be used more effectively during the day.

221 For occasional overnight guests, an inflatable airbed is a comfortable option. Many models include an electric pump for inflating, and they neatly pack away in a dedicated bag when not in use.

222 Purchase a single bed (or daybed) that serves as a sofa by day and bed by night. This is an easy way to provide additional sleeping space for small homes that lack guest rooms.

223 It's possible to add grandeur without intruding on floor space. Large works of art; a floor-to-ceiling bookcase; floor-standing mirrors; and tall, hotel-style headboards enhance a sense of spaciousness.

224 To increase perceived space, elect a headboard that allows you to peek through. A section of wrought iron gate, found in an architectural salvage store, or a contemporary metal frame are good choices.

225 Use the foot of the bed to store the entertainment center—stereo, speakers, and television—with doors that conceal additional storage.

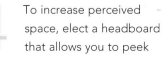

226 If you have a television or entertainment unit in the bedroom that's older than five years, it may be time to replace it. Today's entertainment units are narrower than previous versions as electronic equipment has decreased in size. Opt for a flat-screen TV and save on required floor space.

227 The foot of the bed is a great place to locate a fireplace as well. Even small fireplaces have a big impact in a room. If your space is tight, look for small electric fireplaces and consider recessing them into the wall, leaving floor space open.

228 If building custom cabinetry, measure the items you need to store and build accordingly. If nothing is larger than 11 inches, a cabinet that's 12 inches deep is sufficient.

229 To maximize the size of any room, aim for a minimum of contrast. The palest neutrals—sand, salt, and blush—provide a relaxing environment that is restful and easy on the eye.

design tip

It's important to marry a variety of textures when designing monochromatic spaces. For example, a nubby throw is energized by the proximity of a shiny silk. A sleek tile is enlivened by rustic wood. Aim for contrasts in the weight and feel of materials.

230 The size and impact of pattern you choose for the bedroom is dictated by the mood you want to create. In general, a quiet room contains fewer patterns than a room where the atmosphere is more energetic. If the bedroom is used only at nighttime, consider using minimum pattern in a restful color palette. For those who use the bedroom frequently, a more adventurous mix of pattern may appeal. Keep in mind that pattern takes up more visual space than its absence.

231 In rooms with angles or awkward slopes, consider papering the whole room—walls and ceiling in the same pattern—to distract the eye from awkward proportions. Some wallpaper patterns feature coordinate or matching fabric, particularly effective in creating a cozy bedroom or sitting room. Avoid tiny patterns, which meld into a single color when seen at a distance and look busy when seen up close.

232 Forgo a bed skirt to visually expand the size of the room. Taller legs enhance the illusion.

233   Use sheers on windows to block unattractive views, which may be contributing to a feeling of enclosure.

234   Install bamboo or natural stick blinds to add perceived width to windows.

235   Install blinds above the top of windows to add height to the room's appearance.

236 The greatest space-expanding benefits come from providing a single, seamless color through-out the entire room—and that goes for bedroom flooring, too. To maintain comfort in the bedroom, consider installing wall-to-wall carpet.

237 If the bedroom has hardwood floors, you'll want to add an area carpet for softness. As a general rule, the larger the area carpet is, the larger the room appears. Avoid placing a small carpet just at the side of the bed, as this makes the room feel smaller.

238 If the bedroom has French doors that open onto a balcony, consider placing blinds directly into the doors. Not only does this free up floor space, it makes it easier to use the doors.

239 Enhance the relaxed style in the bedroom by choosing a minimal number of items to display. Choose one large vase to rest on a nightstand rather than multiple collectibles.

240 Choose artwork in the same monochromatic tones to create a restful, seamless color palette and therefore expand space visually, or expand perceived space. A contrasting piece provides an arresting focal point.

design tip
Clutter closes a room in, making it appear smaller.

241 Consider displaying family photos in this personal space instead of other more public areas in your home. A selection of frames in a single color and style helps anchor a family gallery on top of a dresser or shelving.

242 Hang a full-length mirror near or adjacent to a window to amplify available light and expand the apparent size of the room.

1. Measure up from the floor to the desired heights at which you want the top and bottom of the mirror to rest on the door. Draw a level line.

2. Fasten adhesive-backed hooks (or hooks provided by manufacturer) along level lines. Note: If purchasing your own fasteners, consult the weight loads suitable for the product. Also be sure your door is deep enough for the product (some toggle bolts, for example, are too long and require a radius to flip open that is too large for most prehung doors).

243

If wall space is limited, use the back of bedroom or closet doors for full-length mirrors.

3. Place mirror into the hooks.

244 Feng shui encourages a balance of energy to enhance the environment—bringing harmony, peace, and prosperity to the home. In this practice it is recommended not to place mirrors in a fashion in which they reflect your bed, for it is bad luck. To allow the light reflected from mirrors to benefit your room, simply hang mirrors high enough so that they do not reflect your bed.

245 Dark bedrooms are perfect for slumber, but too little light inhibits other activities such as television viewing, reading, dressing, and working. It's easy to assume that small spaces require less lighting; however, like larger rooms, small spaces require an all-encompassing lighting scheme. Every good lighting scheme should incorporate three lighting types: general, task, and decorative lighting.

246 Even, uniform peripheral lighting is ideal for relaxing as bedtime approaches. General lighting sources such as ceiling-mounted fixtures, pot lights, or chandeliers are well suited to this purpose provided they are outfitted with dimmer switches.

design tip
As a rule of thumb, the lampshade should rest at eye level while you are seated.

247 For more direct lighting, position a floor or table lamp beside or behind your shoulder to assist with reading a book or the TV guide. Choose a semi-opaque shade made of pleated silk, stretched linen, or plain parchment to softly diffuse the light.

248 Swing-arm wall lamps on either side of the bed not only provide ideal reading light, they also allow partners to use the lights independently and leave space on the night-stands for a clock, radio, or book.

249 For contemporary rooms, skip the table lamps and consider hanging pendant lamps directly over nightstands. This works well when the bed is centered on a wall, providing a symmetrical composition. Like swing-arm lamps, pendant lights leave nightstands unencumbered.

design tip
To create a romantic mood, fit bedside lamps with colored bulbs—rose or amber.

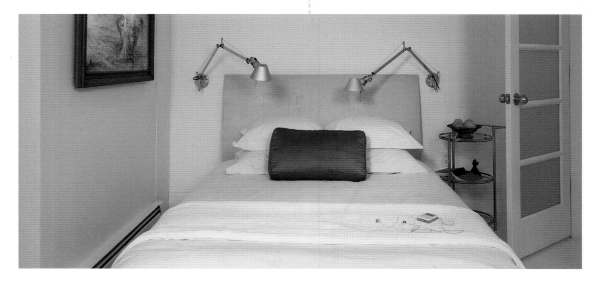

250 Lighting inside and outside the closet area is important. After all, you'll want to see well enough to distinguish between navy and black pants or socks. A surface-mounted light fixture, frequently a long, narrow valance due to the closet's proportions, is the most compact choice.

design tip
Lights that turn on automatically as closet doors open save a few steps on busy mornings.

251 To illuminate a dressing table, especially if this is where you apply makeup, it's important to bring light down near the face rather than coming from above, where it casts unwanted shadows beneath the eyes. Ideally, aim for even lighting on both sides of your face (cross lighting) as this provides the most flattering light for grooming. A pair of table lamps or wall sconces can supply cross lighting. Failing that, a single lamp, preferably one with a flexible arm and head, can be called into service.

design tip
An adjustable lighted magnifying mirror is a must-have addition to the dressing table for those over 40.

252 For tight spaces, multitask your furniture. For example, use a tall chest of drawers or storage tower on one side of the bed to double as a nightstand.

253   Choose a nightstand with closed doors to add storage.

254   Maximize storage capacity of closets with easy-to-install shelving, hanging rods, baskets, and boxes.

255   Use a wicker hamper as both an end table and storage space for blankets.

256 Consider using a built-in along the back wall behind your bed. It then serves as your headboard, nightstand (shelving), and extra storage. Install recessed lights to highlight items displayed on the shelf and to help with light for reading.

257 To save precious floor space, install a single shelf around the room's perimeter one foot below the ceiling. Use the shelf to hold books, baskets with discreet storage, an interesting display, or a combination of all of the above.

258 Purchase an armoire with a tall mirror on the door to double as a closet and provide full-length views and amplified light.

259 An inexpensive MDF round table is a cache of storage once it's covered with a full-length skirt. Use the top for a dressing or bedside table.

260 Chose a bed frame that incorporates storage features.

261 Give the bed a lift and increase storage dramatically. How? Provide a platform with drawers and pullout storage as a perch for the bed.

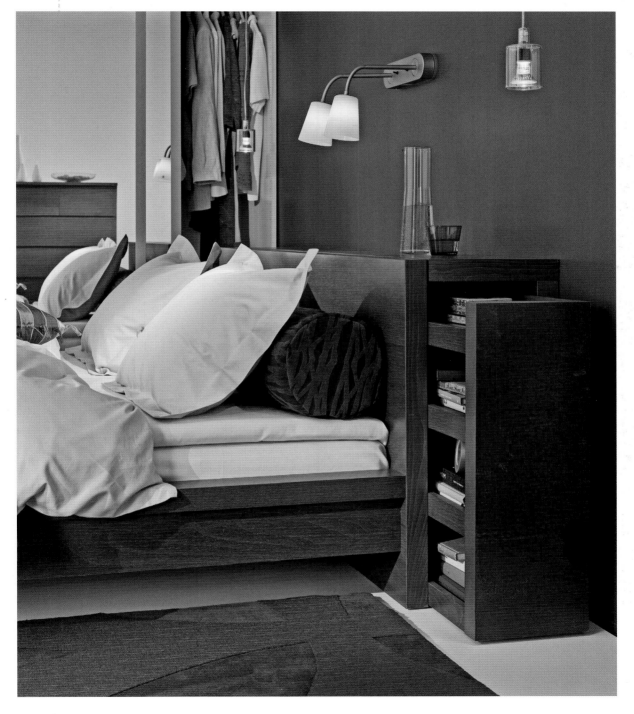

262 Make sure to take advantage of space beneath the bed. As a simple starting point, slide plastic or wicker bins beneath the bed to store out-of-season apparel.

263 If you don't have a closet or significant space for storage, consider installing a floor-to-ceiling closet unit on both sides of the bedroom door's sidewalls. This creates a hallway (of sorts) out of storage that leads into the bedroom proper.

design tip
To free up space in your small home, store out-of-season clothing off-site or in otherwise unused spaces such as the basement or attic.

Case Study

■ A palette of soft yellow and white, enlivened with just a hint of blue, ideally suited my clients' desire for a pretty and gentle master suite. Though I love the sunny vibrancy of yellow, it can be a tricky color to use—too pale and it's insipid, too bright and it's aggressive (rendering a small room even smaller). I settled on Benjamin Moore's Man on the Moon OC-106—a clean shade with real depth, providing the perfect balance of light and intensity. This is an excellent color for bedrooms with some natural light as the pale yellow really glows by daylight. The trim is painted in Decorator's White CC-20 and the ceiling is highlighted in Milky Way OC-10.

By virtue of necessity, a bedroom's main focus is almost always the bed. I fashioned the upholstered headboard after one I'd seen in Los Angeles. Its height commands attention as the room's focal point, and the tufted body (upholstered in pale yellow cotton and linen blend (Kravet #23352-111) accommodates comfortable reading in bed. With fabric-covered furnishings like a headboard, the body may lean or rub against the material, so it's important to use fabric treated for stain resistance.

Sheets and pillowcases in pure white are always the most luxurious choice in my opinion. Darker sheets may contribute to a more dramatic mood, but they do not hold up to frequent laundering the way pure white does. The duvet cover is warmed by the addition of a buttercup yellow bed skirt and small blue accent pillows.

Since comfort and quiet are key considerations in bedroom design, carpeting is a natural choice for flooring. In this case, the neighboring hall carpet features a pale yellow and white trellis pattern, so I opted for solid yellow with subtle texture for the bedroom. Keeping the bed skirt close in color to the carpeting gives the impression of a more generous space.

My clients have a vast art collection, some of it inherited. They were pleased to display four nautical-themed watercolors, two on either side of the king-sized bed, in their new bedroom. The soothing subject matter contributes to the peaceful mood desired. Artwork is perhaps the best way to infuse a room with personality. The mirrored night tables enhance sunlight, add evening sparkle, and reflect the bedrooms new and improved sunny environment.

Dreadful commutes and inadequate or expensive parking options are luring many to work from home. The extra hours of leisure or sleep are an enticing benefit. However, artfully blending two different facets of life—home and work—takes planning and organization.

While a lucky few can afford to devote an entire room to a home office, the majority are limited to small spaces that demand a more creative approach. An adequate workplace doesn't have to be elaborate. It might easily coexist with a guest bedroom, an infrequently used kitchen corner, a dining room that's free all day, or even an underused closet.

home offices

Provided it's thoughtfully designed—allowing for adequate placement of furniture and equipment—even the smallest space can be an efficient place of business. Analyze your needs and be realistic. Do you require separate project-related workstations such as a drafting table or crafts island? If so, you'll need more space than someone who requires only a desk. If you plan to receive clients, you'll want to research neighborhood zoning laws.

Since you may be spending a great deal of time in your newly appointed office, surround yourself with color that enhances your work style. Reds and yellows translate to high energy while cool blues and greens bathe your surroundings in calm. The rewards of a home office are many. Maybe it's time you shortened your commute.

264 An effective home office needn't be large. Allow for a standard-size work surface, 20 inches deep with an 18-inch clearance on each side of a computer, and a comfortable chair.

265 Though a dedicated space is ideal, it's possible to situate an office area within another room. Select a quiet spot, preferably away from other family members.

266 In narrow rooms, position the work surface against a wall rather than floating in the room's center. Standard office units are readily available through popular retailers like Home Depot, IKEA, and Pottery Barn.

267 As in a kitchen, an L-shaped work surface provides a compact and efficient layout. Choose a desk chair with wheels to move easily between adjacent work areas.

268 If you plan to receive clients in your home office, place the desk in the center of the room where it commands attention. Incorporate narrow bookshelves (10 inches deep) on the wall directly behind you. This is the most convenient storage space.

269 Where wall space is limited, consider positioning a desk in front of a window. Allow for adequate window coverings to control glare.

270 A handsome desk and chair that work stylistically with furniture in public rooms, such as the living room or dining room, serve a double duty. Place the desk against the back of the sofa and it will stand in as a serving space for parties.

271 Keep an open mind when looking for office space in your home. With a little creativity, the smallest and most unlikely spaces can successfully function as a home office. For example, consider transforming a wall in a walk-in closet into a home office. Build a desk surface from wall-to-wall within the closet, add shelves above, and select a chair with a low back to tuck completely beneath the desk surface. Close the door and the office disappears from sight.

272 Many use the dining room so infrequently it's a natural to double as the home office. A large buffet can easily hide essentials.

273 Purchase inexpensive shelving and hide it behind full-length draperies. Fabric can hang from a KS track (hospital track). Choose a color that blends with walls for space-enhancing power.

274 If additional workspace is occasionally required, float a work island in to the room's center. This island could be any piece of furniture that is on casters and has significant workspace. When choosing casters consider floor protection, mobility, and the size and weight of the furniture. Here's how to transform any piece of furniture into a multitasking candidate for your home office!

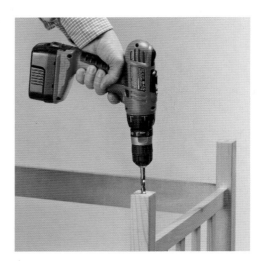

2. Drill holes for the casters, and install the mounting plates with screw.

1. Lay the furniture on its side.

3. Attach the caster according to manufacturer instructions (some are tapped in, while others have threaded holes that screw onto the mounting plate).

275 If you prefer antique furniture, make sure the chair you choose is sufficiently sturdy and its seat height fits comfortably beneath the desk.

276 A large rubber workout ball makes an excellent desk chair, one that enhances posture. It also tucks discreetly beneath the desk when not in use.

277 Purchasing office furniture used to require a trip to the computer store. Fortunately, savvy manufactures are rushing to meet the demands of this growing market, resulting in a wide variety of good-looking desks and chairs that are readily available. Look beyond pieces designed specifically for home offices. An entertainment unit adapts easily to office use as does standard kitchen cabinetry.

278 Consider the addition of vertical file units, approximately 30 inches deep. These stack on top of one another, increasing storage without taxing available floor space.

design tip
Anchor stackable file cabinets to the wall.

279 Provided space allows, a coffeemaker and small refrigerator are worthwhile additions to a home office—and free up space in the kitchen. To keep a small office from feeling cluttered, it's best to conceal these items behind closed doors of a nearby cabinet.

280 Create an instant desk in any room by topping a pair of filing cabinets with a large work surface. Work with a plywood plank wrapped in felt or purchase a laminate countertop cut to size. A simple shelf can be added on top of a radiator for extra workspace as well. There are several retail options for instant desks now as well, often a simple unit to match wall colors are qualities to focus on for small spaces.

281 Choose a glass-topped desk for its space-expanding virtues.

282 Choose a table with a cantilevered shelf to expand your workspace when needed, and to slim down when not in use.

design tip
A wall shelf that has a cantilevered extension also works well. This allows you to keep often-used items on the shelf at all times and expand the work surface when needed. Consider using the shelf for books and writing utensil cups.

283 Small offices frequently have the same technological needs as large offices: namely a computer, fax, printer, phone lines, copier, and software. Measure these items and provide adequate storage for them.

design tip
Choose a laptop rather than desktop computer for its space-saving merits. For maximum comfort, consider purchasing a mouse for use with your laptop at home.

284 Enjoy background music while you work without installing a large stereo system. Purchase a laptop with audio features or convert storage-taxing media into desktop files and upload them onto a handheld media player. If you enjoy antique aesthetics, computer speakers hide well within hollowed antique radios.

285 Resist the urge to keep hard copies of documents. Backup these items on a USB key, which holds a massive amount of data.

286 Learn to use a calendar on your computer and forgo the large paper calendar.

287 A reference library doesn't have to be as extensive as it once was due to Internet resources. Most reputable dictionaries, thesauri, and even atlases now offer complete versions of their physical text copies as online versions. Take advantage of online sources to increase efficiency without taxing storage space. Such attention to detail allows you to use small nooks for your physical home office needs without cramping style.

288 Keep files for one year only. After that, move files into permanent storage. Either rent a storage facility or place them in the garage or attic. Eliminate anything older than seven years (or the time that is in accordance with your local labor laws).

289 An efficient work area requires both ambient (general) and task lighting. To avoid eyestrain, lighting for computer workstations should emanate from above or from the sides of the computer. A small desk lamp is convenient because it is easy to adjust the light to where it is needed.

290 To free up desk space, consider the merits of swing-arm lamps. These are ideal if your desk rests on a wall.

291 Hanging pendants, such as those found over a kitchen island, provide direct light without sacrificing work surface.

292 If custom storage is an option, increase lighting flexibility by attaching lights directly to cabinets.

293 Natural light is always a bonus in the office. To prevent glare without using up precious floor space install adjustable shutters or decorative blinds, as lighting needs change throughout the day. Choose a color that blends seamlessly with the walls and you won't impede on visual space.

294 If the new office space is really a tight squeeze, think vertically. A tower of shelves, wall-mounted bins, and stacking storage boxes take advantage of all accessible space.

295 Decorative crates or baskets store infrequently used catalogues, equipment, or files neatly below the desktop or on top of tall cabinetry.

296 Create separate work stations to define the many functions of a home office, even if you're the one wearing all the hats!

297 Use a trolley for fax machines and printers and wheel it out from storage only when needed.

design tip
Don't overlook the potential of walls to provide additional storage space. An upholstered bulletin board or magnetic strip holds important documents and other communications without cluttering the desk surface.

298 To increase the storage potential of doors and drawers, choose full-extension hardware wherever possible. This type of fitting allows doors and drawers to expand beyond the cabinet frames, bringing their contents into full view. Lower cabinets with drawers or pullout trays are especially useful storage for bulky fax machines and printers. Tucking these items away maintains a clean desktop.

299 Hang clipboards from hooks on the wall to keep tasks clearly in sight and neatly at your side.

300 The humble bulletin board (or pegboard) delivers easy access storage in a busy home office. Paint a pegboard in the same color as the wall and it will blend seamlessly into the background.

301 A small work desk is easily overwhelmed with memos, Post-its, and paperwork. To maintain workspace, stack a series of desktop paper organizers at one side of the desk for notes. To truly save desktop space, strive to keep notes on your computer as much as possible—and get in the habit of using Post-it features for the electronic desktop on your computer.

302 A collection of vintage tins hides an assortment of office supplies such as business cards and stationery.

design tip
Conceal storage space beneath the desk with a tailored skirt. Fit a "slipcover" for the desk with Velcro fasteners, which allows for quick access when required.

303 A small office gains privacy from the simple addition of sliding doors. If you do not have a door to physically close your office at the end of the day, make sure you can at least keep the office out of eyesight and earshot. An easy solution to hide the office from view is to employ a decorative standing screen.

304 Opt for an armoire that has everything you need behind closed doors for your home office. This furniture fits in with the surroundings of living rooms, dining rooms, and even bedrooms.

305 To visually quiet a room and enhance its appearance of spaciousness, avoid overt pattern. A subtle tone-on-tone fabric such as a damask or stripe works well. A more aggressive pattern is better reserved for busier public areas of the home.

306 For a windowless office, consider rich, warm colors such as terra cotta, taupe, and camel. Very pale colors, particularly white, may appear drab without benefit of sunlight. Choose a subtle shift of color for the ceiling, rather than a harsh white. Strong contrast shrinks perceived space.

307 In a home office where sunlight is plentiful, virtually any pale color works well. Pair with a ceiling in white or off-white to amplify sunlight; an asset in any size room.

308 Choose a color palette that supports the work atmosphere you desire. For quiet reading and concentration, choose pale, warm colors such as sisal, coral, and taupe. To create a more dynamic environment, opt for stronger tones in the middle range. Remember, regardless of color, a single unifying palette expands visual space.

309 Whatever unique decorative style you choose, inject your workspace with personality to spark creativity and foster a sense of well-being. You'll want to include a few favorite objects such as treasured collections or family photographs, but don't overdo it. Too many items on display only results in visual chaos.

310 To offer a sense of space and provide breathing room, it's fine to leave a wall blank rather than fill every surface with artwork. Instead, choose designer items for all practical needs, from mouse pads to lights and storage items.

311 Cover computer screens by setting a large table picture frame in front of it when not in use. Tuck the keyboard and mouse under the desk on a pullout tray. These are simple solutions to conceal the office with ease.

312 To improve the acoustic qualities of a home office, opt for full-length draperies and/or wall-to-wall carpeting. To increase the virtual size of the room, choose textiles to coordinate with wall color.

313 If your small office is adjacent to other busier rooms, consider quiet-noise surround sound. Bose makes quiet comfortable headphones, providing soft ambient noise while eliminating outside distractions.

Case Study

■ If you live in close quarters, you don't need me to tell you that every bit of space counts. Recently new clients challenged me to create an office within their open-concept kitchen, dining room, and family room. Ambitious plans included a new wall of built-ins to accommodate storage for dish and glassware, improved lighting, and more comfortable seating for entertaining.

The couple already owned a large sofa and chairs that they wanted to incorporate into the room. Since this area is also frequently used for socializing and entertaining, the office had to be discreet—-in other words, capable of disappearing from view.

The creation of a custom secretary (a piece of furniture with a flip-down desk) within wall-to-wall storage pro-

vided a tidy solution without increasing demands on available floor space. The left side of the unit includes the "secretary," which folds down to create a work surface when needed. In order to maintain a symmetrical appearance, the right side mimics this feature but functions differently. Its mesh door allows air to flow freely around the entertainment equipment housed within. Although the new built-in acts as "office central," the clients are able to use the larger work surface of the kitchen peninsula when space constraints demand.

The cabinetry doors, painted a soft tan to blend with the room's existing features, house the fax, printer, and computer. The "desk chair" resides comfortably within the conversation area when extra seating is required.

By tucking the working elements of the room out of sight, behind closed doors, the mantel finally commands pride of place in this busy home.

Children's bedrooms are often required to accommodate multiple activities—sleep, play, and work. Thankfully, children actually thrive in small bedrooms as they can easily dominate such a space. But finding room for the various tasks required can be a challenge. To further complicate matters, parents and children may have different goals when it comes to the design and decoration of this important space. While easy care, low maintenance, and no fuss are the adjectives that bring every mother joy, a child may have a different wish list when it comes to decorating his or her bedroom.

kids' rooms

Beyond issues of function, which are central, creating an appropriate mood or atmosphere is equally important. A cozy atmosphere is best achieved by choosing warm, soothing colors for main surfaces such as walls and bedding. Coral, pink, and taupe are great choices. Painting the ceiling a shade darker than walls visually pulls the ceiling down, enhancing the desired coziness.

Older children benefit from participation in the decorating process. Incorporating a favorite color or theme may give the child a sense of ownership, encouraging greater care of the space on an on-going basis. For young children, parents may pre-select two options, providing children with a limited choice. Where possible, invest in quality furniture that can grow with your child.

314 It's essential to provide floor space for play, even in the smallest rooms. Placing furniture around the room's perimeter—rather than in the center of the room—increases available floor space.

315 Position a twin bed against the longest wall and put it to work as a daybed. Place deep pillows against the wall for daytime and the bed acts like a sofa. Remove pillows in the evening and the bed is ready for sleeping.

316 A window on the room's narrow side may provide the ideal location for a window seat. The placement of drawers below increases storage space.

design tip
Provided the window is at least five feet wide, the window seat can also accommodate an occasional overnight guest.

317 When it comes to flooring, varnished or painted and sealed hardwoods like maple can take anything your rollerblading, bike-riding toddler can deliver. Add an area rug and you'll dampen some of the inevitable noise.

design tip
To increase the sense of space, choose a carpet that is similar in value (degree of lightness or darkness) to the flooring.

318 A long, narrow room may benefit from wood flooring that is laid horizontally to emphasize the room's width.

319 Sealed cork, popular in Europe for decades, is finally gaining acceptance in North America. Advocates of cork tile love the no-fuss maintenance (sweep and damp mop) and the fact that a damaged tile is easily replaced.

320 Consider the easy-to-care-for merits of linoleum for bedrooms that double as play space. Linoleum comes in 12-foot-wide rolls, making a single sheet sufficiently wide for small rooms. Without seams, it is highly practical and easy to clean, especially in light colors.

design tip
To increase the energy in the room, place tiles on the diagonal. This also increases the perceived width of the room.

321 In small spaces, excessive noise creates discomfort. Look for ways to dampen sound—carpeting, draperies, and built-in cupboards filled with books absorb noise and keep it from translating to adjoining spaces.

322 Children are often more respectful of furniture than adults give them credit for. Introduce vintage or antique furniture into a child's room (where age appropriate) and you'll provide him or her with a meaningful connection to the past and the opportunity to care for a treasured possession.

design tip
Free up space in main living areas by moving one item of furniture such as an armoire or chest of drawers into a child's bedroom.

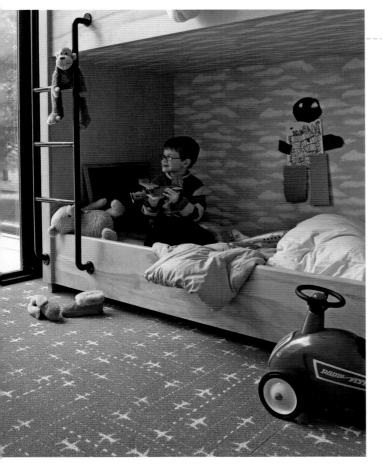

323 Children love sleeping in enclosed spaces; hence the popularity of bunk beds. Stacking beds are ideal for sleeping two children—either siblings or a sleepover friend.

324 Another space-saving option is the niche bed, where sleeping quarters are sandwiched between two layers—pull out drawers below and a ceiling above. In this way, storage can be harnessed from the sleeping space.

325 A trundle bed, with a second mattress that slides from beneath the main bed, is another great option for occasional sleepovers.

326 A loft bed features an elevated sleeping space with a desk or storage beneath, again taking advantage of space that would be lost with a traditional bed.

327

Here's a ditty moms everywhere should memorize, "The higher the sheen the better it cleans." Eggshell might be perfectly fine for civilized living and dining rooms, but children's rooms benefit from a satin, pearl, or semigloss finish.

328

Create a restful atmosphere, conducive to sleeping, by choosing soothing blues, purples, or greens for wall colors. Avoid high-contrast colors that create energy and make a room feel smaller.

design tip
As in other rooms, a monochromatic color scheme is the most expansive in feeling.

329 Slipcovers were invented for moms. Machine washable materials such as cotton or denim are ideal. Aside from the obvious advantages—slipcovers can be tossed into the washer and dryer as often as necessary—these quick-change artists can transform the look of a piece of furniture instantly.

330 Choosing fabrics with the purpose of hiding stains and dirt may sound wise, but the problem with "sensible" patterns is they are so often ugly. Remind yourself that the benefits of having children far outweigh the tiresomeness of cleaning up after them (most days anyway) and choose fabrics that lend a bright and sunny mood to children's rooms.

331 Children thrive in bright, fresh, sunny environments. Paint and fabric colors can help achieve these results, but look for ways to maximize natural light as well. Shiny objects such as brass, silver, crystal, and mirror accentuate light and add luster to rooms.

332 Banish or hide electrical items such as televisions and computers from sight. These items create visual chaos, depriving the bedroom of its restful atmosphere.

333 Mount reading lamps on the wall to free space from night tables.

334 Enhance general lighting with strip lights above bookcases and cabinets.

design tip
The effect of decorative lighting works best when reflected against a crisp white ceiling.

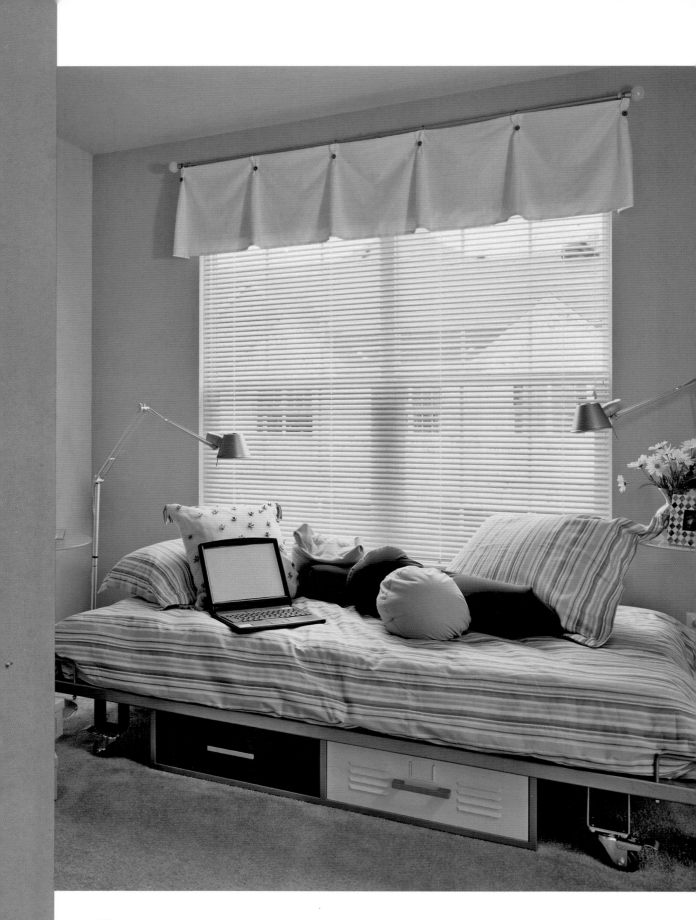

335 Children and adults benefit from an orderly and well-tended environment, so convenient storage is essential. In addition to the usual choices—an armoire to hide electronics or linens, a trunk to hold photo albums or children's toys—you can squeeze extra storage space from existing locations by utilizing the unders: under stairs, under beds, and under skirted tables.

design tip
Use underbed storage options such as plastic bins that slide out of sight.

336 Kids amass a huge collection of toys and books through years of receiving holiday and birthday gifts. Regularly sort through broken or outgrown items and put unneeded or duplicate goods aside for a charity.

337 Every child has beloved toys that are too precious to part with, and you'll want to respect these boundaries. However, if there is reluctance to part with anything, make a deal to store some items in a remote location such as the basement. Agree to check on these items in a few weeks' time and write that date on a calendar. You may discover the child has forgotten all about these items and is now ready to part with them.

338 Evaluate storage needs after a thorough paring down. Purchase storage boxes or large bins from a favorite retailer.

design tip
Allow your child to participate in storage choices. This may encourage him or her to keep the space tidy.

339 Label boxes, bins, and storage drawers; this makes it easier for your child to put things away on a regular basis. For very young children, draw pictures for labels.

340 Provide hanging storage for unusual items like guitars, jump ropes, and large art projects.

341

For young children, the ceiling provides a wonderful canvas on which to enjoy artwork. Soft, billowy clouds or starry skies are popular choices for murals.

342 Although it's tempting to display every work of art your little one brings home, it's actually more rewarding to appreciate them one (or two) at a time. Frame favorite pieces and then rotate artwork regularly.

343 If you can't bear to part with art projects, take a photo of each item. In this way you'll keep a history of art for your child without having to store the pieces themselves.

344 Children love to collect, so provide some storage for favorite groupings. Open shelving is ideal.

345 Deepen a windowsill to hold a collection of potted plants. This is an ideal way to teach your child about gardening.

Case Study

■ We all agree that clutter is one enemy to harmonious living. Like adults, children thrive in an organized, efficient environment—something that is difficult to achieve when a room is overrun with playthings and school projects. Here's how to NIP CLUTTER in your child's bedroom. (These tips work in other rooms as well!)

Name the goal. Before you begin the editing process determine how you want a room to feel and function. For example, a toddler may thrive in a room that's filled with toys and games, so the goal in this case may be to create a dynamic play space. But older children fare better in restful rooms. Determining the desired goal at the outset allows you to make informed decisions along the way.

Take inventory like a business owner—go in search of obsolete, broken, and damaged goods; knick-knacks that have lost their luster; and items in duplicate. Not only are these items taking up valuable storage and display space, on a very real level they contribute to a feeling of disorganization and unmanageability.

Prioritize and gain control. If a toy has not been touched in six months, it may be time to donate it to a worthy charity.

346 Control chaos but enjoy beauty. An absence of clutter doesn't mean a lack of personality. Provided collections and possessions are artfully displayed, they add a welcome, personal touch to children's rooms.

347 Use storage that's integrated into the design of the space. For example, a vintage trunk can act as a bench while discreetly concealing toys.

348 Tend to broken and damaged items. A burned-out light bulb, a broken windowpane, or a door that always sticks robs you of peace of mind and serenity.

349 Children have different storage needs than adults. In order for children to keep their stuff orderly, everything must be scaled to their size. With modular closet systems, baskets, drawers, bins, and even hanging space can be situated low to the ground for easy access. As the child matures, these closet systems can be rearranged.

350 Everything has a place. As usual, my mother was right, but I didn't fully appreciate this until sometime after I'd moved into my own home. After dashing madly about in search of my shoes (I found them in the bathroom) I remembered mom's shoes always went into a basket by the front door.

Entranceways, hallways, landings, and staircases most often provide a physical link between rooms but are frequently treated as an afterthought when it comes to decorating. Since these spaces are visible from main rooms, including them as part of the overall design scheme is essential. While the living room, kitchen, and dining room receive our full attention, the underutilized connecting spaces are frequently ignored. A lack of light, narrow proportions, and high traffic are some of the difficulties we face when dealing with these areas.

entries, halls & utility

When connecting spaces are cluttered and disorganized, other rooms are forced to compensate. Rather than downplay the importance of these hardworking spaces, put them to work. By doing so, connecting spaces take the strain off other more established rooms.

By focusing on decorating a home in a strict room-by-room basis, we may deprive our connecting spaces—the entranceway, hallways, and sister utility spaces like the laundry or mudroom— of the attention they deserve.

Entries

351 Season after season, a well-maintained entrance-way gracefully welcomes family and friends to your home. In fact, it's unlikely that any door in the house gets more consistent use than the front door. Where a formal entranceway is lacking, the door may be the only impression of a proper entrance, so treat it well.

352 Make the front door a distinct color, establishing it as an important element of the entranceway. Again, this is particularly important in small spaces where no real entry exists.

353 Visually emphasize a room's height and distract the eye from limited floor space by papering walls with three-inch vertical stripes. This treatment is ideal for entrance halls as visitors remain standing.

design tip
Stripes that are too narrow—one inch or less—create visual clutter.

354 Wallpaper is the quickest way to provide immediate impact. Opt for diagonal stripes when you want to create energy or excitement.

355 A patterned wallpaper also works well for the entranceway. As this is a transition space—people come and go fairly quickly—it's acceptable to use a bold or dynamic pattern here. This also serves to emphasize the distinct role the entrance plays in the overall floor plan.

356 A side split or center hall floor plan most often includes a prominent staircase. Position a narrow table, small desk, or cozy settee against this wall. The addition of furniture creates the impression of a larger room.

357 Place a narrow console near the entrance door. The handy location is ideal for catching keys, mail, and cell phones as you enter. Select a low profile console (approximately 30 inches high) to give a small entrance an airier look. Top with a mirror to visually expand the space.

358 A desk and chair in the entrance holds keys and mail, and doubles as an occasional workstation.

359 Take advantage of space beside or beneath a staircase. An upholstered chair softens the angular lines of a staircase and may tuck neatly beneath it. A round, skirted table is another excellent choice for entranceways as it also slips—sometimes only partially—beneath the rising staircase. Use the tabletop for display and incorporate a table lamp.

360 An intentional hit of color leads the eye toward a worthy sight while shifting attention from space constraints. Consider placing a Chinese red lacquered armoire or a colorful tapestry at the end of a narrow entrance.

361 Mirror an end wall from ceiling to floor. If you forego baseboards and crown molding on this wall only and butt half tiles (rather than full) up against the mirror, the tiles will become complete with the mirror's help.

362 Many entranceways are plagued with multiple closets and doors. Minimize their appearance by treating the doors identically to the walls. Enhance the walls-only illusion by allowing any molding or wainscoting to run across the closet doors.

363 Further heighten this effect by hanging artwork directly on closet doors. Secure paintings or photos at the top and bottom to prevent banging or bouncing with the movement of the door.

364 Add a chair rail to bare walls, visually expanding the width of the room.

design tip
Avoid placing the chair rail halfway up the wall; the 50/50 ratio is awkward. To create a pleasing proportion, install the chair rail about a third of the way up the wall.

365 Install a full-length mirror on a wall adjacent to a front door with glass panes. This expands the view and amplifies light.

367 If floor space is to remain empty, select flooring with a central medallion. A decorative element that emphasizes the entrance as a distinct room creates the illusion of greater overall space.

366 When choosing flooring, opt for strip flooring that accentuates a feeling of spaciousness. Place strips horizontally (along the width of the room) to visually widen a narrow entrance. To heighten the energy in the space, place strips on the diagonal.

368 As a general rule, larger area rugs create the illusion of a larger space.

369 Avoid an area rug with a border, which draws attention to space constraints.

370

If you have a house alarm or switch box that rests on the entrance wall, it may be possible to hide it from view behind a hinged photo. Choose a print that is larger than the alarm and hinge it on one side, allowing it to swing freely open when required. Most specialty frame shops have the expertise to make a custom frame to fit your needs.

1. Measure the obstacle on your wall.

2. Purchase a hinged frame and hang it on the wall with picture hooks in combination with anchors and machine screws or toggle bolts according to manufacturer instructions. Picture hooks are often sold based on the weight of the object you are hanging. Place hooks along the top and bottom of the frame to prevent it from moving when you swing open the front.

3. When you need access to the obstacle on the wall, simply swing open the front part of the picture frame.

371   Install a rack with shelves above and hooks beneath to hold raincoats, jackets, hats, and mitts.

372 It's always a good choice to provide a seat at the entrance door for sitting down to put on shoes. If possible, look for a bench with hidden storage, ideal for hiding mitts and gloves when not in use.

373 Place an umbrella stand in the corner, but avoid the more visually cumbersome coat rack. If extra coat storage is occasionally required, consider installing a swingout coat hook.

design tip

A traditional piece of furniture such as a chest of drawers, desk, or secretary works well in an entrance-way to hold keys, a desk lamp, and even spillover mitts and gloves.

374 Create a big impression with a small work of art by surrounding it with a generous mat.

375 Make a statement with bold artwork in the entrance. While strong artwork may overwhelm a living room where guests linger, the bold presence is ideal for a transition space.

376 Small pictures hung in rigid order are perceived as one large piece. Tightly group several images together to create a space-expanding impression

Case Study

Umbrella Stand

■ Faced with the challenge of big ambitions and relatively limited floor space, I had to use all my creativity to solve this dilemma: nowhere to place an umbrella stand.

The lack of floor space supplied the impetus for a floating umbrella stand. The wrought iron holder attaches to one side of the closet but straddles both doors, providing the handle by which the door swings open. This is a clever solution that provides storage and frees up valuable floor space.

To minimize the impact of double closet doors, they were painted identically to the walls. The wainscoting features a damask pattern in subtle tones of olive and khaki. A chair rail runs horizontally along the walls and even across closet doors, cleverly concealing them. The chair rail also visually expands the width of the room, eliminating the bowling alley effect frequently seen in narrow entranceways. Artworks hang directly on closet doors.

377

In actuality, very little space is required to navigate a hallway. There is often sufficient space for the addition of a bench or narrow console. For instance, a small
desk turns a four-and-a-half-foot corridor into a mini-office. And don't forget that
the hallway can share its space with other rooms. For example, a bar joining two rooms uses the hallway space for bar seating.

378

Design custom built-ins with no back and eliminate three-quarters of an inch of floor
space. Attach the unit directly to the wall.

379 Narrow stair landings provide just the spot for a slim table or slender display case. Wide stair landings easily accommodate a desk, easy chair, or even a child's daybed.

380 It's tempting to paint narrow hallways in pure white, aiming for an expansive effect. However, an absence of sunlight makes pure white a weak choice. Instead, create a pleasing environment with a pale, warm color such as coral, stone, or oyster.

381 To visually bring the end of a long, narrow hallway closer and therefore make the space appear shorter and more square, paint the end wall a darker shade than the other three walls. For example, choose a pale, cool shade like celadon green on three walls and a deeper leaf green on the fourth wall. Aim for a subtle effect by choosing colors that are closely related in tone.

382 Hallways, especially long, narrow ones, are supremely suited for an artwork gallery. Use the length of the hallway to create a family gallery, displaying favorite photos or a collection of prints or paintings. For sculptures, add a few shelves. To maintain a simple and clean look, avoid shelves with gussets or brackets.

383 Rather than striving to create the impression of more space in a small hallway, why not embrace the intimate scale with strong color. Sometimes a deep orange or royal blue diminishes the impression of limited space by filling the senses with beauty.

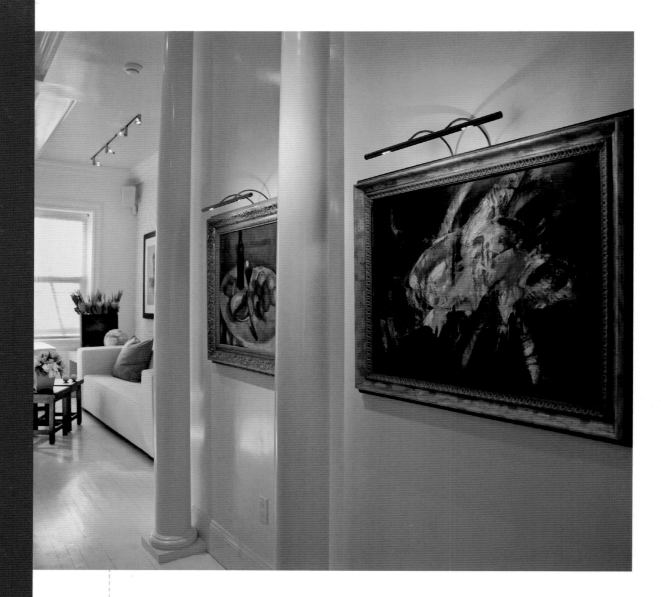

384 Install a series of ceiling-mounted fixtures at regular intervals down a long corridor to emphasize its length. Consider using picture lights and coupling them with photos for a hallway gallery.

385 To emphasize the width of the hallway, install decorative sconces on the end wall.

Utility

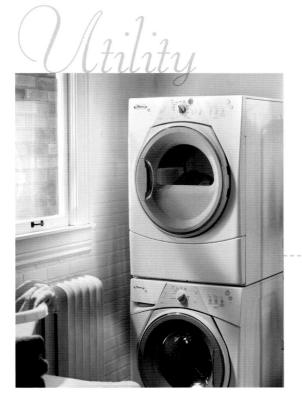

386 Separate the laundry room from a larger utility area with a floor-to-ceiling drape or sliding panels.

387 Opt for a stackable washer-dryer unit when floor space is limited.

388 Call an underused closet into service as the laundry center.

389 Utilize wall space surrounding washer and dryer units by incorporating shelving. For stacked units, consider placing storage towers on either side.

design tip
Include a lower shelf that is at least 20 inches high to accommodate a full laundry basket.

390 As the laundry room is a frequently used space that typically features little or no sunlight, it's best to choose a wall color that is pale and warm. A soft coral or pink adds a pale blush to the room, while a biscuit or stone color offers natural warmth.

391

If possible, include a closet rod (spanning the length of the room) six inches from the wall to facilitate hanging needs. As a compact way to hang clothes, look for swing-out drying arms that fasten to the side of the washing machine.

392

Sorting hampers can ease the workload. Separate whites, darks, and delicates as the laundry arrives. It's possible to hang shelves above these units.

393

A modest four feet of wall space allows for a "mudroom" where none exists. Provide ample storage for boots, hats, gloves, and backpacks, bags, or purses. Dog owners appreciate easy-to-clean surfaces and storage space for brushes and leashes.

394 A compact bench is an ideal perch for putting on shoes. An upholstered cushion provides the most comfortable surface.

395 An effective mudroom frequently operates as a home's main entrance, but it can also be a dumping ground for all the stuff you don't want visitors to see. When that happens, you have an inefficient eyesore instead of a well-functioning utility space. Starting with a well-organized room helps prevent this potential problem.

396 Metal cookie sheets are easily adapted to boot storage for wet weather. Add felt guards beneath to prevent scratching the floor. If possible, slide trays beneath a bench to keep boots out of traffic lanes.

397

Closed cupboards house clothing that is used occasionally while open hooks provide easy access to frequently used items. If custom cabinetry is not an option, place a narrow bench against the main wall and use baskets or cookie sheets to store heavy boots beneath.

design tip
If children require access to hanging space, secure hooks about 36 inches above the floor. Adults will want hooks approximately 60 inches above the floor.

398 Wicker baskets located on an overhead shelf hold scarves, sweaters, and hats.

399 In order to make essentials accessible, space wall hooks about six to nine inches apart; this provides ample room for cumbersome winter jackets.

400 Wooden pegs four to six inches above the floor are terrific for allowing mittens and gloves to dry overnight. Open shelving (or wire shelving) also provides sufficient circulation to aid in drying wet clothing and shoes.

401 Flooring is an important consideration for a complete mudroom effect. Look at floors that are designed for heavy traffic and that are slip-resistant. Ceramic tiles and stone should be honed, a process that removes the high gloss and eliminates the slip factor.

402

Cork and linoleum flooring are hard-wearing and more affordable than natural stone options. As with any space, choose a color that blends with other adjacent colors to expand the room visually.

403

A large mat placed in front of the door not only soaks up slush and water, it also ensnares little pellets of salt and dirt before they are tracked through the house.

It's possible, with some careful planning, to harness outdoor spaces for living. Doing so effectively increases the overall square footage of your home; something anyone living in a small space appreciates. Begin by determining the specific tasks you'd like to tackle outdoors and build "rooms" accordingly. Consider dedicated zones for cooking, dining, reading, relaxing, and playing.

Choose furniture that suits your lifestyle. Many manufacturers carry cast aluminum, synthetic plastic resins, and teak that are suitable for the outdoors year-round. Wicker, though beautiful, requires shel-

outdoor living

ter during inclement weather. Freestanding furniture offers flexibility and echoes the feel of furnishings used indoors. For example, a buffet or teacart accommodates serving and storage.

Create a comprehensive lighting plan with varied light sources. Lanterns and torches provide general illumination while powerful down lights illuminate task areas such as the cooking or eating zones.

Add color judiciously. Choose a neutral palette for furnishings and the beauty of the garden takes center stage. Or go for furniture with bright colors—like red, white, and blue—and then plant all-white or all-yellow flowers in the garden.

No room, indoors or outdoors, can be considered truly personal without the addition of valued objects. A stone sculpture or inviting birdbath increases personal satisfaction with an outdoor oasis.

404 Choose a continuous color palette that flows seamlessly from indoors to outdoors.

405 If possible, continue the flooring from the indoors to the outdoors to enhance the increased space. If you choose different flooring, aim for similar color and pattern for the two choices.

406 As with area carpets, a stone floor situated on grass acts as an anchor to furnishings. The larger the flooring, the larger the space feels.

407 For urban areas that lack grass, consider using AstroTurf for the floor and place plant containers with tall grass around the area.

408 Keep furniture styles consistent with indoor decorating choices to enhance the perceived size of overall space.

409 Install French doors to open interior views to the exterior.

410 Arrange interior furniture with a view of the garden, thus enlarging visual living space.

411 Include mirrors in outdoor spaces to expand views and increase apparent size.

413 Avoid placing chair and sofa backs against windows with a garden view as this obstructs views of the outside and decreases perceived space. Instead, turn chairs to the side to provide a visual path to the largest portions of exterior space.

412 Create a focal point, visible from the inside, in the part of the garden farthest from the house. For example, a freestanding garden shed or section of fencing trained with climbing vines pulls the eye into the distance.

design tip
Use areas below windows for built-in seating and storage. This way your view is maintained, and your indoor space is expanded visually.

414 For homes with out-door settings too cramped for alfresco dining, place a table just inside the doors. A round table allows for easy traffic flow.

design tip
Choose a dining area close to the house to facilitate easy serving, cleanup, and adequate shelter from the wind.

415 A tiny portion of deck, patio, or grass is easily converted into an alfresco dining room.

416 Select a table that complements the scale of the deck or patio. For example, to accommodate a four-foot-diameter table, a minimum 9' x 9' space is required.

417 Where dining space is severely limited, consider a narrow bar to accommodate diners. Counter or barstools slide completely beneath the breakfast bar when not in use. This is a perfect solution for indoor spaces near large windows that open—a clever way to enjoy the fresh air without being affected by rain or wind.

design tip
Explore space-saving options that are available from custom furniture designers.

418 If an outdoor kitchen appeals, opt for an island that supports a barbeque or grill and includes storage space, warming drawers, and even a small refrigerator, depending on budget.

design tip
Situate the barbecue beneath an awning or roof overhang to facilitate grilling throughout most of the year.

419 Sacrifice space for comfort by indulging in luxury. The most popular additions to outdoor spaces are fountains and fireplaces—and these features are available in all sizes, so even a tiny deck can accommodate such a luxury. Be sure to check with local codes before installing these items.

420 Grab valuable storage space within built-in seating and serving counters. Banquette seating maximizes limited floor space and extra-plump seat cushions and pillows are inviting. Likewise, an outdoor island functions much the same way an indoor island does, increasing work and storage space.

design tip
Fire and water evoke a feeling of connectedness to the earth. If space or budget prevents inclusion of a fireplace, opt for a collection of large candles in protective vases.

421 Build an elevated deck and use the underdeck area for storage.

422 Choose fabrics and decorations suitable for outdoor weather. This prevents the need for additional storage.

design tip

Even a slight modification to the pattern alerts people to changes in level, especially important if there are seniors or children in residence.

423   Shade the dining area with an awning, pergola, or umbrella.

424   Shelter seating areas from the elements. Incorporate mature plantings such as tall evergreens to provide privacy, wind blockage, and shade. To create a soft privacy screen, create a floral wall with a fence or trellis covered with climbing roses, clematis, or Chinese wisteria.

425   Select two square tables, rather than a single rectangular table, to increase flexibility of dining space. In this way, tables can be separated to accommodate different tasks.

426 Choose flexible chairs for reading and lounging outdoors. Chairs are easier to move as needed and, unlike sofas, are more easily stored for winter.

427 If a sofa is desired, select a sectional; its individual pieces allow greater flexibility and can be moved more easily into storage.

428 Select fabric colors that blend into the natural environment to maximize the appearance of space. Green, taupe, and soft brown (in other words a brown that is not a dark tone) are easily absorbed into the existing visual environment.

429 As in other rooms, large pieces of furniture create the illusion of spaciousness and provide maximum comfort.

430 Look for furniture that does double duty—a chair and ottoman that accommodate napping, a coffee table that rises up to support dining.

design tip
Choose furniture made of cast aluminum, synthetic plastic resin, or teak for their ability to winter out of doors, thus minimizing storage requirements

Case Study

Increasingly, we demand more from all of our spaces, and the backyard is no exception. A functional and relaxing outdoor living space offers busy family members another location for gathering and a welcome incentive to slow down. Over the years, I've found that careful space planning and attention to design principles work just as well outside as it does inside. One urban backyard provided an opportunity to put that theory to the test.

By building a raised patio we were able to create a seamless transition from inside to outside; simplifying food service from the kitchen to the outdoor table. I chose black cast-iron seating in a classical Regency style. Open chair backs allowed the eye to view the greenery beyond when viewed from indoors. Striped fabric cushions brightened the seating for summertime and were easily stored out of sight during winter.

Rather than positioning one long table to seat the family's six members, we opted for two square tables placed side by side. When more flexible seating is required, the two tables can be pulled apart and used independently. This is a good idea if you are planning on moving homes in the future, as one large table may be more difficult to accommodate than two smaller tables. A large oval umbrella, placed between the two tables rather than through a large rectangular table offers shade to diners.

We created a focal point in the garden beyond by placing statuary within the greenery. A distant focus helps to create a sense of depth in small spaces, even outdoor ones.

431

If storage space is at a premium, look for furniture that opens to reveal hidden compartments.

design tip
Though some furniture can winter out of doors, it's best to store fabrics out of the elements. Look for tables and chairs with lift-up compartments to hide slipcovers close at hand.

432

Extra space is closer at hand than you may think. It is easy to add a room to your living space with the addition of a prefab shack. Convert this shack to a dining room for seasonal entertaining, or add a bed for the occasional guest.

433 For dining on a balcony, use a round table. Smooth edges are easier to travel around.

434 For a long, narrow balcony, place container plantings at both ends of the balcony. The space that is surrendered won't impinge on the main living area and by filling the ends with greenery you create a more pleasing proportion. If possible, hang plantings on the outside of the balcony to provide privacy and color while maintaining space.

435 Place a rectangular table at the narrow end of the balcony. Use the space beneath to hold frequently used items such as a watering can, pinking shears, and barbeque tools.

436 For privacy between balconies, consider adding an architectural salvage wrought-iron piece. Climbing flowers and plants will grow on the piece and provide a soft screen between two balconies.

437 Utilize available wall space (if your condo board or apartment allows) to hang a small fountain. The sound is soothing, particularly in urban settings, and this feature takes up little or no floor space while providing a picturesque focal point.

438 Choose three large containers for plantings, each a different size, and limit plants to these containers. In this way, the plants don't overwhelm the small proportions.

439 Select furniture with open or mesh backs, allowing the eye to wander through furniture to the views beyond.

440 A mirror is a great tool on small balconies. If wall space permits, hang a mirror to reflect views and light into the interior.

It's true that in today's modern homes rooms are often required to provide more than one function. When space is limited to less than 900 square feet, as it frequently is in lofts and condos, the pressure to assign two functions to a single room is even greater. After all, why should a dining room sit unused all week long when it can so easily accommodate a home office, a playroom, or a library?

It's also true that some living spaces are so small it's a wonder they can accommodate one function,

open concept spaces

let alone two. In order to maximize available floor space, many new housing developments feature open concept spaces. In these modern plans, traditional walls and doors are sacrificed in favor of living spaces that merge seamlessly. Without walls to visually impede views, the overall space may appear larger. However, homeowners frequently cite a number of difficulties when it comes to furnishing these spaces. For instance, it's hard to create a distinct role for blended rooms—where does the living room end and the dining room begin?

While it's possible to live comfortably within small spaces, it requires an enormous amount of planning and clever compromise. If you've got big ambitions and limited floor space, this chapter will help you increase the potential in every room.

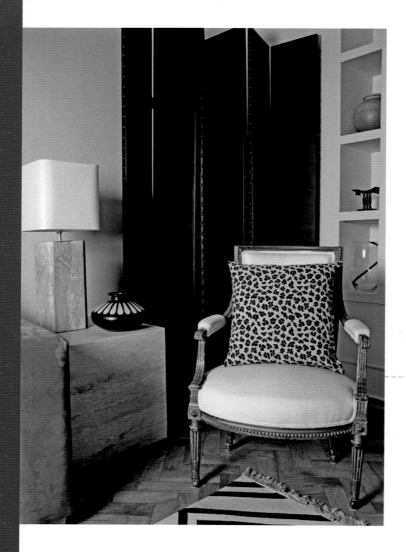

441 Define distinct areas within open concept settings by placing a decorative screen strategically. Positioned between the living and dining rooms, an upholstered or open fretwork screen stylishly divides spaces.

442 A folding screen is well suited to hiding the unsightly from view. This attribute makes it an ideal candidate for a home office area.

443 A folding screen also aids the flow of traffic, directing guests around the entertainment zone, rather than through it.

444 Architectural columns can be employed to define distinct activities within an open concept space. Because these features hug a room's perimeters, they don't impede on visual space.

design tip
For interest, consider upholstering the screen in two fabrics to complement the individual spaces.

445 Half (four feet) or three-quarter height (six feet) walls work well to define and separate one area from another in open concept spaces. Placed deliberately, these short walls maintain the illusion of spaciousness and allow light to move freely between spaces. A low wall positioned beside the entry identifies this area's purpose immediately. Attach hooks to the entrance side of the wall and you'll gain space for scarves and keys to hang unobtrusively.

446 Separate the bedroom from the closet or bathroom area with a freestanding wall. Provide walkways on either side of the wall so anyone using the bed can access the adjacent space conveniently.

447 Opaque or translucent glass dividers define spaces and create privacy. The narrow depth is ideal for areas where floor space is really tight. In addition, they allow light to travel freely between rooms.

448 Sliding glass doors are another great way to divide space into distinct rooms while maintaining a sense of openness. Wall-to-wall dividers are available on ceiling or floor tracks.

449 Use a low bookcase to divide living and dining room. If possible, allow access to books from both sides. Consider topping the unit with a three-inch box cushion to provide additional seating. Or add a stone top to create display space.

450 Hang decorative draperies from the ceiling on a hospital or panel track (a narrow track that affixes to the ceiling). This offers flexibility to close drapes completely, creating a sense of intimacy within individual rooms, or open drapes to stack against the walls, aiding sound absorption and creating a dramatic backdrop.

1. Install the bottom track.

2. Install top tracks.

3. Install drapes.

451 To enclose spaces, use a tall bookcase. This helps to delineate areas but still allows the light between spaces to be shared. Use the bottom shelves for serious storage and the upper shelves for decorative display items or practical purposes such as serving centers or places to set drinks on coasters.

452 Stepping directly into the living room from the front door is disconcerting to guests as it provides no opportunity for adjusting mentally to entering a new space. To remedy, place a folding decorative screen between the entrance and the living room.

453 Another way to delineate an entry where none exists is to place a bench between the entrance and its adjoining room. This low solution maintains apparent spaciousness.

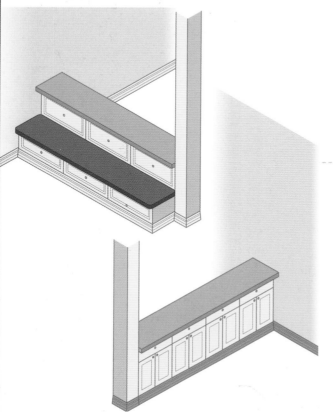

454 Place a buffet back-to-back with a kitchen's storage bench and enjoy an additional serving piece in the dining room with ample storage to hold dishes and stemware. Floating this dual purpose feature between the rooms serves as a mental divide without blocking the room visually. If there are windows in either space, light is able to travel through, creating a brighter shared environment.

455 A change of flooring further denotes an area's purpose. For entries and kitchens, choose a durable floor; and for living, dining, and bedrooms, choose a soft floor. A stone or slate floor (both hardwearing options) is a great complement to wood or carpeting (the latter being a soft option).

456 Use area rugs to define spaces—choose rugs that cover the entire area that is being defined. To help coordinate traffic patterns and designate hallways around the perimeter of the defined space, have rugs stop short of walls.

457 Create an island of conviviality by anchoring a conversation area with an interesting area carpet.

458 When two area carpets are required to lie in close proximity, choose a pair that match to expand visual space. Or when working with complementary area carpets, maintain a disciplined color palette so the effect isn't jarring.

459 Wall-to-wall carpeting provides a seamless flow between adjacent rooms. Select carpet and wall color to work closely together, thus expanding the perceived size of the rooms.

460 It's possible to manipulate the perceived width of a narrow room by laying flooring on the diagonal. This works well in any room, but especially in long, narrow living-dining room combinations.

461 In long, narrow living-dining room combinations, it's best to lay wood planks horizontally, expanding the perceived width of the floor.

462 Maintain a seamless floor between open concept spaces. Where a border is desired, outline the perimeter of the entire floor.

463 Enhance interior views by substituting a solid wall with a see-through window. This technique allows light to travel freely and visually opens up a dark room.

464 Treat windows within open concept spaces identically if possible. The uniformity is a great space expander.

465 When an open space contains a variety of windows (each a unique shape and size) you may be forced to use an assortment of window treatments. Using the same fabric throughout unifies the overall impression.

466 It's possible to modify a built-in bookcase to accommodate discreet workspace. A drop-down table—like those on a secretary—flips open to reveal a conveniently located workstation.

467 Take advantage of any wall-to-wall furniture by building in storage. Take cabinets to the ceiling, if at all possible.

468 When decorating an open concept space, think of it as one room—despite its multitasking personality. A single color palette creates a harmonious whole.

469 Maintain a room's balance by setting pattern around the room evenly. For example, if drapes have a prominent pattern, echo the visual weight by choosing patterned toss cushions for the sofa or chairs.

470 Practice symmetry. A pair of tables, a pair of lamps, and a pair of sofas create visual harmony. This disciplined approach to design generates breathing room, allowing you to incorporate a greater number of items without cluttering the space.

471 Whenever possible, choose midtone wall colors for rooms with dual functions. In this way a room will take on two distinct looks. In daytime, the color appears softer, but it deepens to a duskier shade by evening.

472 One of the largest visual tools is color. By maintaining a single color throughout an open concept space you'll gain perceived footage.

473 Purchase tables and ottomans with concealed compartments. Stash a set of bed linens in a living room that doubles as a guest bedroom or hide table linens in close proximity to the dining room.

design tip
A few of my favorite midtone colors are ICI's Misty Evening #30BG 64/036, a sultry gray blue; Farrow & Ball's Archive No. 227, the perfect stone; and Benjamin Moore's CC-120, a rich camel color.

474   In awkward spaces, determine the primary activity and build around that. Consider traffic routes to avoid guests walking through private areas, such as the bedroom.

475 Rather than accumulating family photos on limited display surfaces, consider installing a family gallery that runs up the wall adjacent to the stairway.

design tip
Follow the ascending angle of the staircase for the most attractive arrangement.

476 Use space above a doorway to hang artwork. Make sure to choose an image that's easy to "read" from that distance. For example, a delicate watercolor may lose some of its charm when seen from below. An abstract or large portrait is a better idea.

477 Use vertical space for storage. To maintain a spacious feel when square footage is slim, opt for open storage. To execute this successfully you must aim for a monochromatic palette—and that means everything from walls to shelving and the items stored in the open must blend together. This allows the items to effectively disappear into the wall.

478 If you have a significant amount of vertical space, build a loft on one long side of the home. This doubles your space on the one side but still allows you to benefit from the vaulting ceiling.

479 To successfully accommodate two functions within a single space, it's essential to provide a flexible lighting scheme. Let's say the dining room also acts as the home office. While a chandelier may provide sufficient illumination for evening meals, dedicated task lighting is required for daytime purposes. Consider each task to optimize lighting.

480 A change of lighting helps distinguish distinct functions within an open concept space. For example, a chandelier may hang above a dining table, while a living room may rely on pinpoint spot lights and table lamps.

481 Keep pathways and traffic lanes within an open concept space free from obstruction. Overtaxing these areas produces visual confusion and emphasizes the lack of space.

482 Furniture that does double duty—a coffee table that rises to eating height or a futon that provides space for daytime seating and night-time sleeping—serves to maximize the potential of every room.

483 Situate a desk behind a sofa and it doubles as serving space for parties.

484 Place a low (approximately 30 inches high) bookshelf perpendicularly between the living and dining rooms. Or place a pair back-to-back to serve each room independently. The shelves provide much-needed storage and display space.

design tip
Consider placing a pair of table lamps on either end of low bookshelves to provide additional lighting. This idea requires an adjacent electrical outlet to work. If none exists, add a pair of hurricane lamps—readily available at retailers like Restoration Hardware, Pottery Barn, and Crate and Barrel.

485 Position a daybed between the living and dining rooms. This serviceable piece of furniture provides seating, facing any direction—ideal for parties. In a pinch, the daybed comfortably accommodates an overnight guest. Some designs incorporate a second bed that pulls out from under the daybed, doubling the guest beds you have to offer.

486 A regular complaint from those who reside in open concept homes is the noise factor. Without traditional walls and doors, noise is amplified; a problem exacerbated by the hard surfaces of flooring, cabinetry, and countertops frequently found in main areas. To increase audio comfort, install broadloom or lay area carpets to dampen noise from foot traffic and absorb other sounds.

487 Another way to dampen sound is to install a white noise system. Electronics that create white noise are widely available. You could also mask creaks or echos with a small bubbling water fountain.

488 Opt for floor-to-ceiling draperies rather than metal, mesh, or wood blinds.

489 Layer the room with textiles—upholstered seating, cushions, and hanging tapestries soften the sound environment.

490 Choose quiet appliances.

Even a shoebox-sized home can support an efficient, clean, and beautiful kitchen. Use a closet for a small kitchenette. Hide away the kitchen by pulling down a roll-top door.

492 A closet is also an ideal location for a quaint sitting area. Small nooks make for perfect reading spots.

493 Consider forgoing a traditional dining room in favor of a low Japanese-style seating arrangement. In this way, the living room doubles as the dining room.

494 To maximize space, select pedestal furniture—including tables, buffets, and chairs.

495 With increasing frequency, families are choosing to include dining space within the kitchen, freeing the proper dining room to function as needed. As long as minimum traffic allowances are observed, a dining table is nearly always a welcome addition to even the smallest kitchen.

496 To gain additional seating in the kitchen, add a second counter made of glass above the traditional island top. Raise the second counter by six inches and extend it over the island to provide knee space for bar stools.

497 The more available light in an interior, the larger that room feels. Consider adding transom windows, small hinged windows above doorways—sky views visually open horizons.

design tip
Select a round table for tight quarters; it's less likely to interfere with traffic. The addition of leaves in the center creates an oval shape when expanded.

498 Place a narrow rectangular table against an available wall to seat a pair of diners. If required, the table can occasionally be pulled away from the wall to accommodate extra guests.

499 Consider pulling materials from outdoors into the interior. For instance, if the deck is made of slate, continue that material inside; if wood siding is used outdoors, pull the siding onto interior walls. The shared element visually expands views.

500 Place a shelf on top of a radiator—or create an L-shaped shelf that begins with the radiator but turns the corner. Tuck a bench or footstool beneath the new surface and you've acquired some modest workspace or an interesting display area.

Case Study

Defining Space; Adding a Mudroom

■ A hardworking mother with three children challenged me during her kitchen renovation to provide space, no matter how small, for a mudroom. The small urban home afforded no obvious location for the children's backpacks, jackets, and schoolwork. An addition, due to budgetary constraints, was simply out of the question. However, a frequently used side door that led from the backyard into the kitchen provided a suitable location for just such a feature.

I started by designing a half wall (three feet high) to rest perpendicularly between the kitchen proper and the new mudroom; providing a clear perimeter to the new 3' x 4' area. A change from the wood flooring of the kitchen to a more serviceable slate tile emphasized the change of function. A storage bench against the wall offered a perch for changing boots and shoes. Directly across from the bench a narrow coat cupboard was placed. Inside, high bars accommodate adult coats while low hooks make it easy for children to hang books and backpacks.

Although the homeowner sacrificed some square footage within the kitchen, the new mudroom was an invaluable addition and a worthy resale investment.

resources

California Closets
800-274-6754
www.CalClosets.com
p. 165 (left)

Bonaldo
Bonaldo SpA
Via Straelle, 3
I-35010 Villanova (PD)
+39/049/9299011
Email: bonaldo@bonaldo.it
www.Bonaldo.it
p. 14 (bottom), p. 54 (top), p. 59 (bottom),
p. 154 (bottom), p. 164 (bottom)

Bristol Design
p. 40 (bottom)

elfa ® International
elfa ® North America
800-384-3532
www.elfa.com
p. 196 (top)

FLOR
Inspired modular floor covering.
1-866-281-3567
www.FLOR.com
p. 69 (bottom), p. 76 (bottom), p. 101 (right), p. 102, p. 150 (top), p. 153 (bottom), p. 156, p. 160 (bottom), p. 178, p. 197, p. 200 (bottom), p. 203 (bottom), p. 207

hANdwerk
Unique high quality environmentally friendly
flooring out of Austria
Shown: Rollywood rollout wood flooring in
Maple and Beech with textured surface.
702-882-5632
www.hANdwerk.us
p. 23 (bottom)

IKEA Home Furnishings
610-834-0180
www.Ikea-USA.com
p. 1, p. 30, p. 35, p. 38 (top and bottom), p. 43 (top and bottom),
p. 41, p. 46 p. 58 (bottom), p. 95 (top), p. 123, p. 124, p. 134 (bottom), p. 155, p. 157 (top and bottom), p. 159 (top and bottom), p. 162, p. 164 (top), p. 165 (right), p. 190, p. 191, p. 226 (bottom)

Kimberly Seldon
Kimberley Seldon Design Group
416-780-9187
www.KimberleySeldon.com
p. 11, p. 13 (top), p. 15, p. 17 (top), p. 20 (bottom), p. 29, p. 33 (bottom), p. 36 (left), p. 37, p. 49 (top), p. 50 (top), p. 55 (top and bottom), p. 56 (bottom), p. 60 (right), p. 73, p. 80 (bottom), p. 85 (bottom), p. 86 (left and center), p. 125 , p. 139 (top), p. 141 , p. 147, p. 87, p. 88, p. 89 (right), p. 91 (right),
p. 92 (left), p. 93 (right), p. 99 (right), p. 100 (top), p. 101 (top), p. 106, p.136 (top), p. 163, p.170, p. 180 (left and center), p. 181 (right), p.183,
p. 193, p. 211, p.224 (bottom), p. 231 (right), p. 235

Kitchoo Systems (France)
13 Chemin du Levant
01210 Ferney Voltaire
www.Kitchoo.com
p. 33 (top), p. 36 (right), p. 38 (top), p. 40 (top),
p. 41 (bottom), p. 50 (bottom), p. 232

Lofty Ideas
www.loftyideas.ca
Ideas, suggestions, and tips for open-concept spaces.

Modern Spaces
415-357-9900
www.ModernSpaces.com
p. 108 (top and bottom)

Natasha Kapij Design
781-929-8077
www.NKInteriorDesign.com
p. 107 (bottom)

Plato Woodwork, Inc.
Plato, MN 55370
800-328-5924
p. 195 (bottom right)
p. 48 (right) / © photo Pat Sudmeier for Plato Woodwork, Inc.

Poggenpohl
+49-5221-381-0
www.Poggenpohl.de
p. 47 # KI 89 photo courtesy of Poggenpohl

Room and Board
800-301-9720
www.RoomAndBoard.com
p. 12 (top), p. 69 (top), p. 110 (top), p. 120, p. 121 (top), p.127, p.133, p. 135 (bottom), p.138, p.141 (bottom), p. 220 (top) p.234

Ruhl-Walker Architects
617-268-5479
www.RuhlWalker.com
p. 218 (top)

The Sliding Door Co., Inc.
888-433-1333
www.SlidingDoorCo.com
p. 218 (bottom)

Sol-R
800-567-7657
Hospital ("panel") tracks.

Teragren
Fine Bamboo Flooring, Panels & Veneer
800-929-6333
www.Teragren.com
p. 233 (bottom)

Tulikivi
+358-0207-636-000
www.Tulikivi.com
p. 10, p. 26

photograph credits

p. 3 / photo Shelley Metcalf, Shelley.Metcalf@cox.net (619-281-0049), design William Bocken AIA Architect / Interior Designer BBocken1@cox.net (619-260-1162)

p. 6 © Brand X Pictures

p. 08 / photo Arcaid / Alamy

p. 8 (top) / photo © Karen Melvin, design Senn & Youngdahl Fine Builders

p. 9 / photo © Tony Giammarino / Giammarino & Dworkin

p. 11 / photo Ted Yarwood, design Kimberly Seldon Design Group

p. 11 / photo © Jessie Walker Associates

p. 12 (bottom) / photo © Tony Giammarino / Giammarino & Dworkin

p. 13 (bottom) / photo © Tony Giammarino / Giammarino & Dworkin

p. 13 (top) / photo Ted Yarwood, design Kimberly Seldon Design Group

p. 14 (top) / photo © Karen Melvin

p. 15 / photo Ted Yarwood, design Kimberly Seldon Design Group

p. 16 / photo kolvenbach / Alamy p. 17 (bottom) / photo © Jessie Walker Associates

p. 17 (top) / photo Ted Yarwood, design Kimberly Seldon Design Group

p. 18 / photo © Jessie Walker Associates

p. 19 (bottom) / photo © Jessie Walker Associates

p. 19 (top) / photo Mark Samu

p. 20 (top) / photo © Karen Melvin, design Arteriors, Tim Bjella Designer

p. 20 (bottom) / photo Ted Yarwood, design Kimberly Seldon Design Group

p. 21 / photo Lindsey Stock / Alamy

p. 22 / photo Mark Samu

p. 23 (mid right) / photo Ted Yarwood, design Kimberly Seldon Design Group

p. 24 / photo © Jessie Walker Associates

p. 27 / photo © Jessie Walker Associates

p. 28 / photo © Jessie Walker Associates

p. 29 / photo Ted Yarwood, design Kimberly Seldon Design Group

p. 32 / photo Elizabeth Whiting & Assoc. / www.ewastock.com

p. 33 (bottom) / photo Ted Yarwood, design Kimberly Seldon Design Group

p. 34 (top) / photo Brian Vanden Brink Photographer © 2006

p. 36 (left) / photo Ted Yarwood. Designer, Kimberly Seldon Design Group

p. 37 / photo Ted Yarwood, design Kimberly Seldon Design Group

p. 42 /photo © Arcaid / Alamy

p. 48 (left) / photo Tim Street-Porter / Elizabeth Whiting & Assoc.

p. 49 (bottom) / photo © Tony Giammarino / Giammarino & Dworkin

p. 49 (top) / photo Ted Yarwood, design Kimberly Seldon Design Group

p. 50 (top) / photo Ted Yarwood, design Kimberly Seldon Design Group

p. 53 / photo © Beth Singer

p. 54 (bottom) / photo Brian Vanden Brink Photographer © 2006

p. 55 (bottom) / photo Ted Yarwood, design Kimberly Seldon Design Group

p. 55 (top) / photo Ted Yarwood, design Kimberly Seldon Design Group

p. 56 (bottom) / photo Ted Yarwood, design Kimberly Seldon Design Group

p. 56 / photo Elizabeth Whiting & Associates / Alamy

p. 57 / photo © Jessie Walker Associates

p. 58 (top) / photo Brian Vanden Brink Photographer © 2006

p. 59 (top) / photo © Jessie Walker Associates

p. 60 (right) / photo Ted Yarwood, design Kimberly Seldon Design Group

p. 60 / photo © Eric Roth

p. 62 (bottom) / photo © Karen Melvin, design Locus Architecture, Minneapolis, Wynne Yelland & Paul Neseth

p. 61 / photo Corbis Premium Collection / Alamy

p. 61 / photo Elizabeth Whiting & Associates / Alamy

p. 62 (top) / photo Mark Samu

p. 63 / photo Beateworks Inc. / Alamy

p. 64 / photo 122 Fotolia © Stephen Coburn / www.fotolia.com

p. 65 / photo Mark Samu

p. 65 (right) / photo © Karen Melvin, design Rottlund Homes

p. 66 / photo Ted Yarwood, design Kimberly Seldon Design Group

p. 67 / photo © Karen Melvin, design Sawhill Kitchens

p. 69 / photo © Tony Giammarino / Giammarino & Dworkin

p. 70 (top) / photo © Tony Giammarino / Giammarino & Dworkin

p. 70 (bottom) / photo © Karen Melvin, design Henderson House designed by Jeff DuCharme

p. 71 (bottom) / photo © Jessie Walker Associates

p. 72 (top) / photo Shelley Metcalf, Shelley.Metcalf@cox.net (619-281-0049), design William Bocken AIA Architect / Interior Designer BBocken1@cox.net (619-260-1162)

p. 73 / photo Ted Yarwood, design Kimberly Seldon Design Group

p. 75 / photo Niall McDiarmid / Alamy

p. 76 (right) / photo Mark Samu

p. 76 © Brian Vanden Brink

p. 77 / photo Studio Liquid / Alamy

p. 78 / photo Brand X Pictures / Alamy

p. 79 (top) / photo David Giles / Elizabeth Whiting & Assoc.

p. 79 / photo Beateworks Inc. / Alamy

p. 80 (bottom) / photo Ted Yarwood, design Kimberly Seldon Design Group

p. 80 (top) / photo © George Gutenberg / Beateworks / Corbis

p. 81 / photo © Eric Roth

p. 82 (bottom) / photo © Beth Singer

p. 82 (top and bottom) / photo Arcaid / Alamy

p. 83 / photo Niall McDiarmid / Alamy

p. 84 / photo © Eric Roth

p. 85 (bottom) / photo Ted Yarwood, design Kimberly Seldon Design Group

p. 85 / photo Key Collection / real. / Alamy

p. 86 (center) / photo Ted Yarwood, design Kimberly Seldon Design Group

p. 86 (left) / photo Ted Yarwood, design Kimberly Seldon Design Group

p. 86 / photo © Eric Roth

p. 87 / photo Ted Yarwood, design Kimberly Seldon Design Group

p. 88 / photo Ted Yarwood, design Kimberly Seldon Design Group

p. 89 (left) / photo Mark Samu

p. 89 (right) / photo Ted Yarwood, design Kimberly Seldon Design Group

p. 91 (left)/ photo Key Collection / real. / Alamy

p. 91 (right) / photo Ted Yarwood, design Kimberly Seldon Design Group

p. 92 (left) / photo Ted Yarwood, design Kimberly Seldon Design Group

p. 92 (right) / photo Mark Samu

p. 92 (right) / photo Mark Samu

p. 93 (right) / photo Ted Yarwood, design Kimberly Seldon Design Group

p. 94 / photo © Eric Roth

p. 95 (bottom right) / photo Arcaid / Alamy

p. 95 /photo © Dana Hoff / Beateworks / Corbis

p. 96 © Brand X Pictures

p. 97 (bottom) / photo Beateworks Inc. / Alamy

p. 97 (top) / photo Elizabeth Whiting & Associates / Alamy

p. 98 © Brian Vanden Brink for Hutker Architects

p. 99 (right) / photo Ted Yarwood, design Kimberly Seldon Design Group

p. 100 (bottom) / photo Elizabeth Whiting & Associates / Alamy

p. 100 (top) / photo Ted Yarwood, design Kimberly Seldon Design Group

p. 101 (top) / photo Ted Yarwood, design Kimberly Seldon Design Group

p. 102 / photo Lu Jeffery / Elizabeth Whiting & Assoc.

p. 103 © Brian Vanden Brink forJohn Colamarino, Architect

p. 105 / photo Mark Samu

p. 106 / photo Ted Yarwood, design Kimberly Seldon Design Group

p. 107 (top) / photo © Karen Melvin

p. 107 / photo by Edua Wilde Photography / for Collinstock.com. Photographed in the South End neighborhood of Boston, MA.

p. 109 (bottom) / photo Lindsey Stock / Alamy

p. 109 (top) / photo Niall McDiarmid / Alamy

p. 110 (bottom) / photo Beateworks Inc. / Alamy

p. 111 (bottom) / photo Arcaid / Alamy

p. 111 (top) / photo Arcaid / Alamy

p. 112 (bottom) / photo Elizabeth Whiting & Assoc. / www.ewastock.com

p. 112 (top right) /photo Elizabeth Whiting & Associates /Alamy

p. 112 (top) / photo 230 Fotolia © auris / www.fotolia.com

p. 113 (bottom) / photo Mark Samu

p. 113 (top) / photo © Tony Giammarino / Giammarino & Dworkin

p. 114 / photo Corbis Premium Collection / Alamy

p. 115 (bottom) / photo 240 Fotolia © Galina Barskaya / www.fotolia.com

p. 115 (top) / photo Beateworks Inc. / Alamy

p. 116 (top) / photo © Karen Melvin, designCarol Belz and Assoc. Interior Design

p. 116 (bottom) / photo Steve Hawkins / Elizabeth Whiting & Assoc.

p. 117 (left) / photo Beateworks Inc. / Alamy

p. 118 (left) / photo 246 Fotolia © Stephen Coburn / www.fotolia.com

p. 119 (bottom) / photo © Eric Roth

p. 119 (top) / photo Shelley Metcalf, Shelley.Metcalf@cox.net (619-281-0049), design William Bocken AIA Architect / Interior Designer BBocken1@cox.net (619-260-1162)

p. 121 (bottom) / photo 255 Fotolia © Dóri O'connell / www.fotolia.com

p. 122 / photo Arcblue / Alamy

p. 122 / photo Arcblue / Alamy

p. 125 / photo Ted Yarwood, design Kimberly Seldon Design Group

p. 128 (bottom) / photo © Jessie Walker Associates

p. 128 (top) / photo Brian Vanden Brink Photographer © 2006

p. 129 / photo Brian Vanden Brink Photographer © 2006

p. 130 / photo © Todd Caverly 2007, Peter Bethanis Architect

p. 131 (bottom) / photo Brian Vanden Brink Photographer © 2006

p. 131 (top) / photo © Jessie Walker Associates

p. 134 (top) / photo © Eric Roth

p. 135 (top) / photo Arcaid / Alamy

p. 136 (bottom) / photo © Beth Singer

p. 139 (bottom) / photo Brian Vanden Brink Photographer © 2006

p. 139 (top) / photo Ted Yarwood, design Kimberly Seldon Design Group

p. 140 / photo © Karen Melvin, design Randall Kipp AIA

p. 141 © Brand X Pictures

p. 142 (both) / photo Brian Vanden Brink Photographer © 2006

p. 143 / photo © Jessie Walker Associates

p. 144 (bottom) / photo Arcaid / Alamy

p. 145 (both) / photo Brian Vanden Brink Photographer © 2006

p. 146 (left) / photo Elizabeth Whiting & Associates / Alamy

P. 146 (left) / photo Mode Images Limited / Alamy

p. 146 (right) /photo Elizabeth Whiting & Associates / Alamy

p. 147 / photo Ted Yarwood, design Kimberly Seldon Design Group

p. 149 / photo © Tony Giammarino / Giammarino & Dworkin / design Christine McCabe

p. 150 (bottom) / photo Key Collection / real. / Alamy

p. 151 (top and bottom) / photo Brian Vanden Brink Photographer © 2006

p. 152 (top) / photo Stock Connection Blue / Alamy

p. 153 (top) / photo © Jessie Walker Associates

p. 154 (top) / photo © Karen Melvin, design Andrea Waitt

p. 158 / photo © Beth Singer

p. 160 (top) / photo © Karen Melvin, design Andrea Waitt

p. 161 / photo Enigma / Alamy

p. 163 / photo Ted Yarwood, design Kimberly Seldon Design Group

p. 164 / photo Brian Vanden Brink Photographer © 2006

p. 166 / photo Jon Bouchier / Elizabeth Whiting & Assoc.

p. 168 (bottom) / photo Elizabeth Whiting & Assoc. / www.ewastock.com

p. 168 (top), / photo Mark Samu

p. 169 / photo Mark Samu

p. 170 (lower left) / photo Mark Samu

p. 170 / photo Ted Yarwood, design Kimberly Seldon Design Group

p. 171 (left) / photo © Jessie Walker Associates

p. 171 (right) / photo Mark Samu

p. 172 / photo Shelley Metcalf, Shelley.Metcalf@cox.net (619-281-0049), design William Bocken AIA Architect / Interior Designer BBocken1@cox.net (619-260-1162)

p. 173 / photo VIEW Pictures Ltd / Alamy

p. 173 / photo VIEW Pictures Ltd / Alamy

p. 174 / photo Andreas von Einsiedel / Alamy

p. 175 / photo Niall McDiarmid / Alamy

p. 176 (left) / photo Arcaid / Alamy

p. 176 (center) / photo Mark Samu

p. 177 (right) / photo doug steley / Alamy

p. 180 (left and center) / photo Ted Yarwood, design Kimberly Seldon Design Group

p. 181 (right) / photo Ted Yarwood, design Kimberly Seldon Design Group

p. 182 (bottom) / photo Tom Leighton / Elizabeth Whiting & Assoc.

p. 182 (top) / photo Brian Vanden Brink Photographer © 2006

p. 183 / photo Ted Yarwood, design Kimberly Seldon Design Group

p. 184 / photo Mark Samu

p. 185 (top) / photo Mark Samu

p. 185 / photo Neil Davis / Elizabeth Whiting & Assoc.

p. 186 (left) / photo Beateworks Inc. / Alamy

p. 187 (right) / photo Mark Samu

p. 188 / photo © Eric Roth

p. 189 (bottom) / photo Brian Vanden Brink Photographer © 2006

p. 192 / photo Mark Samu

p. 193 / photo Ted Yarwood, design Kimberly Seldon Design Group

p. 194 (left) / photo Brian Vanden Brink Photographer © 2006

p. 194 / photo © Jessie Walker Associates

p. 195 (right) / photo Brian Vanden Brink Photographer © 2006

p. 196 (bottom) / photo © Karen Melvin, design Ginny Anderson Architects

p. 199 / photo Shelley Metcalf 619-281-0049, Shelley.Metcalf@cox.net

p. 200 (top) / photo Beateworks Inc. / Alamy

p. 201 / photo Mark Samu

p. 202 / photo Key Collection / real. / Alamy

p. 203 (top) / photo Gary Chowanetz / www.ewastock.com

p. 204 (bottom) / photo Shelley Metcalf, Shelley.Metcalf@cox.net (619-281-0049), design William Bocken AIA Architect / Interior Designer BBocken1@cox.net (619-260-1162)

p. 204 (top) / photo Key Collection / real. / Alamy

p. 205 (left) / photo Key Collection / real. / Alamy

p. 206 / photo Greg Vaughn / Alamy

p. 208 (bottom) / photo Nicholas Pitt / Alamy

p. 208 (top) / photo Nicholas Pitt / Alamy

p. 209 / photo Arcaid / Alamy

p. 210 / photo Shelley Metcalf, Shelley.Metcalf@cox.net (619-281-0049), design William Bocken AIA Architect / Interior Designer BBocken1@cox.net (619-260-1162)

p. 211 / photo Ted Yarwood, design Kimberly Seldon Design Group

p. 212 (left) / photo Lise Dumont / Alamy

p. 212 (center) / photo Ian Fraser / Alamy

p. 213 / photo © Lise Dumont / Alamy

p. 213 / photo DAVID EASTLEY / Alamy

p. 215 / photo Shelley Metcalf, Shelley.Metcalf@cox.net (619-281-0049), design William Bocken AIA Architect / Interior Designer BBocken1@cox.net (619-260-1162)

p. 216 / photo Lindsey Stock / Alamy

p. 217 (bottom) / photo Arcaid / Alamy

p. 217 (top) / photo Elizabeth Whiting & Associates / Alamy

p. 218 / photo by Edua Wilde Photography / for Collinstock.com). Photographed in the South End neighborhood of Boston, MA.

p. 218 / photo by Eric Lamph Photography for Sliding Door Co.

p. 219 / photo VIEW Pictures Ltd / Alamy

p. 221 / photo Arcaid / Alamy

p. 221 / photo Niall McDiarmid / Alamy

p. 222 / photo Andreas v. Einsiedel / Elizabeth Whiting & Assoc.

p. 223 (top) / photo Peter Cook / VIEW Pictures Ltd. / Alamy

p. 223 (bottom) / photo Pieter Estersohn / Beateworks Inc. / Alamy

p. 224 / photo © Todd Caverly 2007, Judy Ostrow designer

p. 224 (bottom) / photo Ted Yarwood, design Kimberly Seldon Design Group

p. 225 (top and bottom) / photo © Tony Giammarino / Giammarino & Dworkin

p. 226 (top) / photo Shelley Metcalf, Shelley.Metcalf@cox.net (619-281-0049), design William Bocken AIA Architect / Interior Designer BBocken1@cox.net (619-260-1162)

p. 227 / photo Arcaid / Alamy

p. 227 / photo Beateworks Inc. / Alamy

p. 228 / photo Niall McDiarmid / Alamy

p. 229 (top) / photo Jeremy Cockayne / Alamy

p. 229 (bottom) / photo John Edward Linden / Alamy

p. 230 (top) / photo © Eric Roth

p. 230 / photo Beateworks Inc. / Alamy

p. 231 (right) / photo Ted Yarwood, design Kimberly Seldon Design Group

p. 233 (top) / photo © Beth Singer

p. 233 / photo Elizabeth Whiting & Assoc. www.ewastock.com

p. 235 / photo Ted Yarwood, design

index